Letter to my Father

Letter to my Father

Words of love and perspectives on growing up from sons and daughters

EDITED BY FELIX CHEONG

Published in 2021 by Marshall Cavendish Editions
An imprint of Marshall Cavendish International

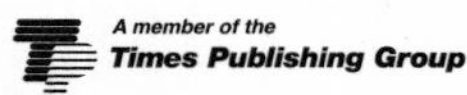

Other Marshall Cavendish Offices:
Marshall Cavendish Corporation, 800 Westchester Ave, Suite N-641, Rye Brook, NY 10573, USA • Marshall Cavendish International (Thailand) Co Ltd, 253 Asoke, 16th Floor, Sukhumvit 21 Road, Klongtoey Nua, Wattana, Bangkok 10110, Thailand • Marshall Cavendish (Malaysia) Sdn Bhd, Times Subang, Lot 46, Subang Hi-Tech Industrial Park, Batu Tiga, 40000 Shah Alam, Selangor Darul Ehsan, Malaysia

National Library Board, Singapore Cataloguing-in-Publication Data

Names: Cheong, Felix, editor.
Title: Letter to my father : words of love and perspectives on growing up from sons and daughters / edited by Felix Cheong.
Description: Singapore : Marshall Cavendish Editions, [2021]
Identifiers: OCN 1242598853 | ISBN 978-981-4928-78-6
Subjects: LCSH: Children—Correspondence. | Fathers. | Father and child.
Classification: DDC 306.8742—dc23

Printed in Singapore

Cover design by Adithi Khandadai

This book is dedicated to all parents,
in the hope that these shared experiences will
inspire and shape your own parenting journey.

Contents

Foreword

Felix Cheong

For most of us, having a frank chat with your father seems to be one of the hardest – if not the hardest – things to do, right up there with getting an audience with the Prime Minister. Unlike mothers, regarded as more nurturing (and thus closer to the heart), fathers are distant, almost like a satellite revolving on its own centrifugal force around the family.

You are, of course, connected to him by love, but it is perhaps best experienced at arm's length.

After all, the father figure – at least in a traditional Asian family – is the provider, the protector and the policeman. Add the archetypal image of a man as being strong and silent, and it is little wonder communication channels with our father are not always clear.

In this companion anthology to *Letter to My Mother*, 20 contributors have been invited to reopen communication lines with their father. For some of them, their letter is an expression of long-overdue gratitude for his years of upbringing. For others, their letter seeks solace in absence, in what they have missed about their late father. And for a handful, their letter is a coming-to-terms with an absent father, one whose leaving had left them bereft and undone.

I, too, had had my fair share of stop-and-start conversations with my father. It was only in the last few years of his life that we took to talking more often. Even then, we had our differences and sometimes, it got the better of us (it did not help that I take after him in being quick-tempered). I always thought there was time enough to make peace and make it up to him.

Even when Dad was hospitalised for pneumonia in December 2019, I clung onto the hope there was tomorrow, and a daisy-chain of tomorrows, for all the things I wanted to tell him.

No – too little, too late. Just three hours after I visited him briefly at Changi General Hospital, he left. The last thing he had whispered to me (pneumonia had all but robbed him of his voice) that afternoon: "I want to sleep." And he did.

My eulogy for Dad, which I read, while choking back tears, at his funeral three days later, was the most difficult poem I have ever written. Difficult, not because it was stylistically challenging, but because it gathered feelings that I had never told him about:

In Memoriam Dad (1940 – 2019)

You slipped away on Thursday evening
When the machines they hooked you up to
Were not paying attention.
Every line, flat as death.
No getting away from facts.

When I saw you, you looked so alone in sleep
Not even God's thunder, as Mum would joke,
Could rouse you (being hard of hearing
Was hardly an excuse).
Your body was tilted towards the window,
Like mimosa to light,
Waiting for the sun
To open the petals of your spirit.

Who were you, my father?
You were an angry young man
Who bottled the rage of the 60s
And uncorked it in every job you ever held
(And sometimes on our buttocks when mischief
Got the better of us).
Maybe that was why jobs
Never held you long enough in any one place.

You were a printer's apprentice
Who rolled out miles of stories in newsprint.
How apt my career would run a parallel course
As reporter and poet, making track in stories.

That Thursday afternoon, you had pointed out
How my face had appeared in a *Straits Times* ad.
You couldn't speak (pneumonia had robbed you
Of your tongue) but the pride in your eyes
Was more than enough for me.

Later, your doctor would tell me how
You had mentioned it to him too.
And I remember your stash of newspaper clippings,
Collected like a miser over 20 years,
Of every story about me ever published.

I don't know if you recall,
But you had been training me since I was 12 for this.
Remember how I helped you draft (and type) your job applications?
I was a hungry reader and that was proof enough for you
I was a good enough writer.

You had beautiful penmanship, every cursive line
Like a gentle flourish,
The occupational hazard of a printer taking pride
In how words are presented.
I must have picked up this trait
For students would sometimes tell me
(When I'm not annoying them
Or annoying to them)
They like my handwriting.

You were a messy and picky eater.
You were stubborn to a fault, stubborn by default.
You made a Worker's Party supporter out of me.
You were a warden in church who gave
And prayed generously
Because you feared God in the only way Catholics knew how.

You were Mum's strength
The past 12 years when ill health
Spun the joy out of her life.
You were indefatigable, organising
Her medical appointments (and your own)
The way a secretary does.

But your devotion was also your weakness.
You refused to see how your own body
Had weakened, week by week,
Organ by organ.

Dad, I had taken you for granted for a long time,
More times than I fear I will remember.
I was angry with you, curt, abrupt, even hostile.
There were times I even hanged up the phone on you.

There is now no time left on the clock
To make it up to you.
And because I'm a lapsed Catholic
Who half-believe in the afterlife,
I will never be able to.
And for this, I will ever regret.

I had dedicated my first book of poetry to you and Mum
But I've never written about you.
This poem is my last testament to make up for lost time
But not the loss of you.

The sun is out today, after a week of chill and rain.
It is a glorious day
For a man to meet the Son of Man.
Goodbye, Dad. Your deadline is here, your story has been filed.
Let the printer begin rolling
Reams of prayers and thank yous.

Felix Cheong is the author of 19 books, including six volumes of poetry, a trilogy of satirical flash fiction and five children's picture books. His works have been nominated for the prestigious Frank O'Connor Award and the Singapore Literature Prize. His latest work is a libretto written with composer Chen Zhangyi, *Panic Love: An A Cappella Opera,* released as a music video.

Felix (right) and his late father.

Conferred the Young Artist Award in 2000, Felix holds a Masters in Creative Writing and is currently a university adjunct lecturer with the National University of Singapore, University of Newcastle, Murdoch University and Curtin University.

I Wonder What You Would Say

Margaret Thomas

Dearest Pa,

It is late at night as I write this here in my cluttered little study. Behind me and to the side are shelves stuffed with books, some of which I may never get around to reading. On other shelves are piles of files, stacks of old notepads and paper for recycling, boxes of this and that, and yet more books.

It occurs to me that I could be describing your study, the space you always had for yourself in the three houses we lived in over the years, homes that were rich with the laughter and the little melodramas of our Peranakan extended family life.

But where the insulated mug of iced water stands on my desk, you would have had a bottle of beer or a glass of wine or a pot of tea. And where my laptop and large second screen sit, you would have had your Adler typewriter. And I live alone. So, it is the same, but a little different.

The cool night breeze has become stronger and the half-closed louvre blinds are flapping, so I get up to adjust the angle of the slats, and I stand a while at the window of my 24th floor flat and look out. It is peaceful at this time. Most people are asleep, but there are lights everywhere – streetlights, traffic lights, the lights in corridors and other public spaces of buildings. And there are buildings all around and far into the distance – Ang Mo Kio and beyond.

In the 1959 General Election, this was the area that made up much of the Thomson constituency. There would have been few lights visible then at this time of night. There were mostly just villages, farms, and plantations around here, with unlit and uneven dirt roads.

The 1959 General Election was the one election you contested in the 10 years or so that you were in politics, and you stood in the Thomson constituency. I was just eight then and did not really know what was going on, but I remember how a small crowd of your supporters turned the back patio of our house in Rosyth Road into a poster-making factory, nailing pieces of cardboard onto wooden stakes and then slapping on the glue and carefully positioning the paper posters on the cardboard.

I have a vague memory of going with Mum to one of your election rallies. It would have been somewhere out there in the now built-up areas that I see from the windows of my flat in Upper Thomson.

You were an Englishman, albeit one who had been a Minister in the Labour Front government since 1955 and who had become a Singapore citizen in 1957, standing in a constituency that was rural with mostly Chinese-speaking voters. So, you asked us – your Chinese wife and half-Chinese daughter – to come on stage with you, presumably to show voters your connection and your commitment to Singapore.

Our appearance at that rally might well have gotten you a few extra votes because, while you did not win the election, your 28.3 per cent share of the vote in the three-cornered fight was better than that of the candidate who was Chinese. He got just 17 per cent of the vote. The winner, with a 54.6 per cent share, was Indian.

In your autobiography *Memoirs of a Migrant*, you wrote: "Race has always played a very small part of elections here. The voters have shown again and again that they are willing to vote for someone who is not of their race and does not speak their language."

Reading that passage makes me wonder what you would have said if you had been here in 1988 when the GRCs (Group Representation Constituencies) were introduced on the grounds that the minority races might otherwise not get elected to Parliament. And I wonder what you would say whenever the ruling party declares, as it does with some regularity, that Singapore is not ready for a non-Chinese prime minister.

But you left us in 1977. You were just 65, and I was 25. Perhaps if your sarcoma had been diagnosed early enough, it could have been treated more effectively and we might have had more years with you. More years for me to get to know you as a person and not just as my father. More years for you to see some of the paths that I ended up taking in life.

I wonder, for instance, what you would have said when I left the Monetary Authority of Singapore, or MAS, after two years and became a journalist. I think you would have approved. Journalism has a greater parallel with the profession you ended up in, that is, teaching, than with being the investment analyst that I was supposed to be at MAS.

Like you, I had no idea what I wanted to do after university, and consequently began my working life in an area I was totally unsuited for. It was beginning to dawn on me, and more importantly on my MAS bosses, that I was better at working with words than with helping to manage Singapore's reserves when the journalism job appeared.

I cut my teeth as a journalist mostly writing editorials for *The Business Times*, which was great training for the column writing I would go on to do and which led me onto the other path that I think you would approve of, that of civil society activism.

It was the columns with a feminist slant that I wrote for *The Singapore Monitor*, the English-language daily newspaper which had a pitifully short life of about three years in the mid-80s, that led to my being invited to be a speaker at the 1984 forum that was the genesis of the gender equality group AWARE, or the Association of Women for Action and Research.

The women's movement was well under way in the UK when I was a postgraduate student in London in the mid-70s. I usually bought a copy of *Spare Rib*, the monthly magazine put out by a group of feminists in London, but I did little more than read the magazine, or parts of it at least. This must have had some impact on my views, but I do not recall spending much time thinking about feminism and gender equality.

I also do not recall talking about these issues with you when I was back in Singapore in 1976. But we did not really have very much time together. Not long after I got back, you went off to London with Mum and Ann to find an explanation for the persistent pain you were having in your hip. The explanation we got was not one we wanted to hear, and after that we were all on a bit of an emotional rollercoaster.

We might not have talked about feminism, but I know what you would say about AWARE and its work; you would be completely supportive. Your views are there in some of your talks and articles.

In 1971, you spoke at Fairfield Methodist Girls' School about higher education and careers for girls. You said: "Generally on paper, careers are equally open to women and men; but the realities are not quite the same. Women, until recently, were a kind of second-class citizen in most, or even in all, countries of the world. Today, they may be equal in principle, but some careers will offer them better prospects than others."

And in a 1969 article titled "Women for Priesthood", you wrote: "If we privately think of women as inferior men or superior animals, we shall not be able to accept them as priests. This is a real objection. Jesus did not take women into his 12 Apostles: The primitive society of his day would have rejected them, and Christianity with them.

"But women watched his death on the Cross and went with his body to the tomb. After the Resurrection, he showed himself first to a woman. The Gospels do not teach us that women are unfit to handle the body and blood of Christ. If we find them unfit, the fault is in ourselves, whether we are men or women."

I know you would be fully behind AWARE's declared mission, which is a society where there is true gender equality – "where women and men are valued as individuals free to make informed and responsible choices about their lives".

Yes, I know that point about valuing people as individuals would have had your wholehearted support. A theme that comes up again and again in *Memoirs*, in your speeches and articles, is your frustration with bureaucracy, with the structures and systems that reward conformity and stifle individuality, initiative and creativity.

As a teacher and principal, you were always much more concerned about the laggards and the misfits, the naughty boys, the rebels, the forgotten and the misunderstood. In *Memoirs*, you say: "We must NOT close our minds and hearts to the needs of those who do not neatly fit the schemes of our changing society. The schemes change rapidly; what we reject today may be the keystone of the next thing we have to build."

Singapore today is in a better place than it was in the 70s for this. There is more room for those who do not conform, more acceptance of differences, more recognition of the value of diversity and the importance of inclusion.

But we still have a long way to go, as can be seen in the recent case of the transgender student whose co-ed school appears to be insisting that she present and behave as male when in school, even though she has the support of her parents and doctors to start the transitioning process.

You were the principal of a boys' school, so it was unlikely you would have had to deal with such an issue. In the 60s and 70s, when you were Principal of St Andrew's Secondary School, I doubt that there would have been many cases of gender dysphoria among minors whose parents were supportive of their transitioning. Sexuality and gender identity were not things that were very openly discussed in those days.

But I know that you saw the need for sex education in schools. In 1967, you announced at the school's annual speech day: "Students ought to get some properly planned teaching and guidance in sexual matters, both physiologically and socially, and that is what we hope to arrange."

So, I wonder what you would say if you were here today, both about the transgender student's case and also about the little protest that a few young people staged in front of the Education Ministry because they were upset about the authorities' lack of clear support for transgender students. Three of the protesters were arrested and several others questioned. It is not clear at this point whether they face charges.

I suspect the schoolmaster in you would say that if there is a law against such protests, then the police should apply the law. But I would like to think that you would support the call for clarity by the authorities on the matter, and that if you were the Education Minister and you were aware of the protest, you would have come down and defused the situation by asking the protesters to join you in a meeting room and hearing them out.

It is when I am reflecting on these kinds of situations that I often think of you, and wonder what you would have to say about them. You were, in many ways, a man ahead of his time, and I dearly wish you could see some of the progress we have made in the last 44 years.

I thought of you in July 2020 as I was reading the endless stream of messages in chat groups and posts on social media that were analysing and commenting on the outcome of GE2020.

You died in October 1977. A year earlier, in December 1976, I sat with you in our living room to watch the TV coverage of the results of GE1976.

The PAP had held every seat in Parliament for a decade because the main opposition party, Barisan Socialis, decided in 1966 to boycott Parliament to protest Singapore's split from Malaysia. The 1976 General Election saw a contest in nearly every constituency, but the PAP won 70 per cent of the vote and swept all seats.

As the Returning Officer, on election night 1976, again and again declared the PAP candidate the winner, your disappointment was palpable. It was not because you were opposed to the PAP. You admired what Lee Kuan Yew and the PAP had done for Singapore, but you believed Singapore needed a viable opposition if it were to have a future.

A week or so after the election, you wrote a paper titled "A Government, no Opposition, and the Future". The Singapore government, you said, was amongst the best in the world, but "we cannot surrender the future entirely to the contingency planning of the backroom bureaucracy". A loyal opposition would have "real differences of intelligent opinion and be able to make a real change in the conditions of life without wrecking the state".

Your paper, which you said you had meant to send to a small circle of friends, essentially argued a case not just for a viable opposition, but for more Singaporeans to take an interest in what was going on and to be ready to participate in one way or another in policy-making and politics. In other words, for a strong and vibrant civil society.

"At present, too many of us are like the giraffes and hippopotami in our Zoo, or the birds in the Bird Park; our needs are foreseen and provided for, we can be the

Margaret with her parents, Francis Thomas and Catharine Lee Eng Neo, 1959.

admiration of visitors from less happy lands; but we lack the ability and scope to plan for ourselves", you wrote.

I do not know if you ever sent this paper to anyone. You were grappling with cancer and might have decided to just focus on writing your account of the dying days of the Labour Front government which had preceded the PAP government. You were, of course, a founder member of the Labour Party of Singapore, and later a nominated Minister in the Labour Front governments under the leadership of first, David Marshall and then, Lim Yew Hock.

In July 2020, as I digested the implications of GE2020, I wanted to be able to turn to you and say: "It has taken us a few decades, Pa, and there were many obstacles to find our way around. But we now have the beginnings of that viable opposition you wanted to see. And there is a vibrant and growing civil society. I think we will be okay."

Margaret Thomas was a journalist for more than 25 years at *The Business Times*, *The Singapore Monitor*, SPH *AsiaOne* and *TODAY*. She now works primarily on book projects and, in various voluntary roles, on the pursuit of gender equality and an open, informed, and inclusive society. She was a founder member of AWARE (Association of Women for Action and Research) in 1984/85 and is its current President. She has also been involved in civil society organisations and initiatives such as TWC2, the Singapore Women's Hall of Fame, and the Singapore Advocacy Awards.

My Love Letter to My DD

Sadie-Jane Alexis Nunis

Being an only child has its benefits, as it does its tribulations. I know, how very dramatic. Honestly, with both you and Mummy – and I am not just saying this because it is on paper – it has been a rather sweet ride.

The only downside is that though I am getting older and moving on to a new decade, come April 2021, I am still your overgrown baby. I know this, as you have never failed to remind me of it. I love it 99 per cent of the time but sometimes, I really do need both of you to see me as the grown-up that I am.

Though I was born in Singapore, I did not stay in Singapore for the first few years of my life, not that I really remember any of it. I still recall being told that my Dd was instrumental in starting up Malaysian Airlines (I also remember how your heart broke when you see or speak about what has since become of the airline).

We moved back to Singapore as both you and Mummy felt that it was better to be based in Singapore – honestly,

I never really found out why but it had led me to my journey, right?

You then became a hotel consultant, then Managing Director/Chief Executive Officer of various multinational companies. I hardly saw you as you were away two-thirds of the year.

Mummy often told me that you had worked hard as you wanted to give me a good life. The plus point about you holding the various positions meant that I always got what I wanted, unless Mummy got in the way of it.

When you were in town, you would take me to Toys "R" Us and, because of your connections, I managed to be the first in Singapore to get my Pound Puppy. I still keep it today, as it is a sweet memory. I remember you pushing me around in the big Toys "R" Us trolley, row by row, asking me to choose whatever I wanted. Sometimes I did, but most times, I spent the money at MPH and Times bookstores while you and Mummy shopped at Robinsons when they were all housed at The Centrepoint.

Mummy told me that you would try to coincide at least one trip a year with my school holidays so that we could travel with you. In this way, I have travelled to a lot of interesting places and stayed in suites and enjoyed VIP treatment. Mummy rolls her eyes whenever she tells me stories about how I would pout and ask why I was not in the first-class seats with you. She would then shake her head as you would then switch seats with me. Okay, fine, there were times when I was a tad spoilt – but only with you and Mummy.

Though I was spoiled rotten, I do not think I am a spoiled brat. Mummy made sure of it and you were assured that she would. You gave me lots of moolah when I went to school (though Mummy had kept the bulk of it in my savings account – boo!).

Material-wise, it was great. Even as a child, I carried luxury goods (though I was not one to flaunt it). As you kept up with gadgets because of work, you ensured that I had the same, though I was but a student then. I know my mobile phone bills were insane as they went into the four digits. I also know that you would grumble to Mummy about this but when she nagged me, then told me that you were mad at me, all I needed to do was bat my eyelashes and pout. Time after time, you would just pat my head and melt, saying: "Do not do it again." Repeat this *modus operandi* for the next decade or so.

You were very welcoming of my buddies, even chilling with them when they came over; paying for their petrol (you felt sorry for them as they were all schooling), and taking them to the country clubs for dinner. Sadly, these same buddies have disappeared from my life.

Why do I keep talking about all this? Because I know that this is how you, my dear Dd, showed his love. I know that many a time, you felt guilty about not being able to be there most days, or even months, when I was growing up. It meant that you missed a lot of key moments in my life. Your way of showing your love and affection for me is very old school – through actions, versus through saying it.

I know you were proud, shocked, and a little sad when you saw all my certificates that I had earned from primary school onwards, when you were filing my documents for when I was to go for the Australian fair. Sad, because you had missed seeing me receive these awards; proud for the obvious reasons; and shocked, because they filled up box files.

You know, now that I reflect as I am penning this, I think even till today, it is only on Father's Day, your wedding anniversary, Easter, Christmas, and New Year's Day, that I hug my Dd. Given that the years are getting shorter, maybe the hugs should be more frequent and longer.

Honestly, I cannot remember the last time I told you that I love you either. I think that I, too, show love through actions instead of words. Oh, and the goodbye or hello kisses that I give you when you drop me off at my meetings or events.

In fact, I think – no wait, I *know* – that we are more alike than I would like to admit. Admittedly, you are definitely way smarter and more talented than I am. I was told that you think that I am brilliant. But when I lay it out and compare, the fact that you can still remember how to play your guitar while singing (albeit slightly rusty), versus me on my bass, shows there are still more things you supersede me, Dd.

One talent that I envy is how you can draw, whereas I have trouble differentiating my drawing of an apple and a heart. I have these vivid images in my mind but I am unable to translate them onto paper. That is one talent I wish I had.

You are fluent in Malay and Bahasa Indonesian (to the point that you could actually lecture in these languages) and you can also speak Tamil. I mean, come on, Tamil? It still tickles me pink whenever you explain to shopkeepers in Tamil how they have calculated the bill wrongly, though, frankly, I doubt that they pay attention as they gawk, being more intrigued by how this man rattles off in their mother tongue.

Another thing that we are more alike in, though I wish it was not so, is our fiery tempers. There are times when we have gone to war with each other, and have said things that we should not have. Given that we both have a stubborn streak as well, many a time, these fights have gone awry, and bitterness ensues. We go from zero to nuclear in a matter of seconds.

Do I regret these arguments? Yes, obviously, right?

Another similarity: We both have egos, or maybe it is more a matter of pride than anything else when it comes to admitting our mistakes to each other.

However, the one who has to apologise, is always me. Why? Why should I if I did not do anything wrong and it was you who were in the wrong? Why do I have to succumb? I am a grown adult, so why am I still treated like a baby?

Simple. Because Mummy says that you are my father and I have to respect you.

Many a time, I have to grit my teeth. Thank God for mobile phones and texting, as the times that I do not wish to be the first one to wave the white flag, I just text one word: Sorry. After sending you that one-word text, I simply stew in my grumpiness and anger.

You know it, too, more often than not, as you would soften and offer to make me noodles as your version of a peace offering, or offer to drive me somewhere (even if Jerrid has already offered).

The plus point is that we are both not petty people; so, soon afterwards, the war is forgotten and we move on.

My memories with you are few. This is ironic, given that I remember most things.

The memories that I do have are of how we both used to volunteer at Sacred Heart Church when we used to go there. You were a warden, while I was in the choir and also a lector/commentator.

I remember how you used to take me on double-decker bus rides on weekends when Mummy had to work (this was before she stopped work to look after me); after which, we would have breakfast together. I cannot recall, sadly, what we spoke about, given that I was a smallie. However, I assume that we both had fun as we did it for a long time.

I remember how you used to send me to school whenever you were in town. I also remember how many of my friends used to giggle and tell me that you reminded them of Hollywood actor Richard Gere. Cue a mixture of pride and wanting to gag – all at once.

I remember how you set up my visit to the Istana in Johore as I wanted to meet a real-life princess. You do not like asking for favours but you did – just because I had asked.

I remember us going to visit Grandma in Ipoh, how I first saw you cry when she was being cremated. I remember telling Mummy: "Now Dd is an old orphan." But I also told you that you still have Mummy and me as I stood beside you, holding your hand.

I remember how you took leave on the day of my 'O' Level results. That was the first time that you had made time to follow me to pick up my results. I remember feeling anxious, nervous, and yet relieved that you told me no matter what, you would be proud of me.

I remember how you made the effort to head up to Melbourne for my 21st birthday and how you hung out with my friends and me. Usually, Mummy would be the one but you had wanted to make me feel extra special, so you came instead.

I remember how I saw you tear for the second time when I was awarded my degrees. Thankfully, these were your happy tears of pride. I was told that you were proud of me all the other times too, just that you were not always there to relish those moments.

I remember how I got a tad annoyed that I had to rush from an appointment to bring you to hospital as you had tummy pain. And I remember feeling absolutely guilty for feeling that way when I found out, years later, that it was misdiagnosed. It was actually your first heart attack. I only found this out when you had your second heart attack.

I remember almost blacking out when I found out that your heart was not functioning well and you needed a bypass operation. I remember being worried with Mummy when we saw you in the ICU and then the High Dependency Ward, after being told that you had to go through a quadruple bypass.

I remember your look of disappointment when one day, I brought home the love of my life. It was not because he was not worthy, but because it happened so suddenly and out of character for me. I remember your disappointment as you felt that I was committing a sin by living together.

I remember the effort it took to win both you and Mummy over to accepting Jerrid. I remember our fun times in Kuala Lumpur when you, Jerrid, and I hung out together while Mummy met her friends.

I remember your anxiety whenever I have my specialist appointments or get hospitalised when I have various relapses for my illnesses. I remember you saying to Jerrid: "You do not need anyone else, the four of us. We are all the family that you need." By that, I knew you have already accepted Jerrid.

I remember both of you looking older as you worried about my health. I remember commenting to Jerrid how much you had aged over the last five years as we watched you walking ahead of us. I remember the pang of sadness as I know that the day will come.

I remember our various car rides, when it was only the two of us and we would be swinging between two extremes, either talking non-stop or sitting in silence and just enjoying the music.

I cannot wait to remember your look of pride when (and if) I next graduate, achieving my ultimate goal of getting my doctorate.

I am sorry for the time wasted on the arguments, for getting grumpy or annoyed with you when you cannot help but have grumpy old man syndrome (all men get grumpy when they get old – ha ha).

I cannot wait for you to walk me down the aisle. I am sorry that I will never be able to give you grandchildren. I have always felt this is where I have failed you as a daughter.

Sadie-Jane with her father Gerard Nunis, circa mid-1990s.

Thank you for never forcing marriage or children on me. Thank you for being ever supportive of everything I do. Thank you for always being there and being someone that I can count on. Thank you for accepting me for everything I am. Thank you for loving me.

Will I ever show this letter to you? I honestly do not know. Thinking about it, I feel a tad awkward, even shy. I cannot explain why.

For now, I will stick to my hello and goodbye pecks on the cheek, the pecks during the sign of peace at mass, and our yearly hugs. And hope that by the time you read this, it will not be too little, too late.

Dr Sadie-Jane Alexis Nunis is SIM's Head Librarian and Editor of quarterly senior management E-magazine *Today's Manager*. Sadie-Jane sits on various councils–Secretary: Singapore Kindness Movement Council; President: Library Association of Singapore (2021–2023); Member: Asia-Pacific Business School Librarians' Group; Member: Council of Chief Librarians; President: Deakin Alumni (Singapore Chapter); Member: Singapore Business and Professional Women's Association; and EXCO Member (2020-2022): Federation of Business and Professional Women (Singapore).

She holds a double degree in Journalism and Public Relations; an MBA; and recently completed her Doctorate in Business Administration, focussing on Marketing and Consumer Behaviour.

She has a life, she swears!

A Letter to My Father

Christina Thé

My dear, beloved Pa,

I shall start this letter with a story about a boy:

She was to name their newborn the "Golden Mountain", a name he bequeathed on his deathbed. Next to the dying young man stood his heavily pregnant wife and their two daughters. Their youngest, still a baby herself, had barely started walking. The wife promised to carry out his wish.

But the elders said: "This name is too heavy for him!" A name too grand, too boastful, for such a poor family.

Maybe the elders had a point. The baby was not even born yet. They did not even know if it was going to be a boy, or if it would survive at all. It was not an easy time, post-war; they were Chinese migrants who barely got by for food.

But the child's father insisted. That was to be his last wish. That was all he could leave them with. A hope.

"My love, I am sorry," he said with his dying breath.

He had gazed upon her the very first time when his parents had gone to ask for the hand of a girl neighbour whose house was across from hers. The young man waiting outside had watched this girl sweeping her veranda. She was about 15, with rich, wavy hair reaching her shoulders; petite, yet with curves in all the right places.

The young man marched into the house where his parents were making small talk with the intended family and the matchmaker. He announced he preferred that girl across the street instead. His parents and the matchmaker were mortified.

Many profuse, apologetic bows later, and much reprimand of their son, they acceded to his request and moved the party across the street.

"Have you made up your mind this time? Don't ask us to move to another house again, ah, son. So embarrassing," the parents had berated him. Not that he cared.

The girl's parents, though, had had reservations; the young man was considered much older, being in his mid-20s. He assured them that would not be a problem. Indeed, they lived happily as a couple. He made a living as an electrician, while she looked after their growing family – until tragedy struck. The smallpox epidemic ravaging their city took everything from them. Their youngest son would never meet his father.

***

I can only imagine how his wife must have struggled after his passing; a young seamstress in her early 20s with three little mouths to feed, plus the loyal old nanny, Mbok Mie. She told me every time it rained, she would carry you, Pa, with one arm, while the other, armed with her thick wooden clog, would be busy smacking the army of little scorpions rising out of the water.

I guess *Oma* (Grandma) really did not have much of a choice when she gave you and your sisters up to the orphanage. How hard the choice she had had to make as a mother, to part with her children to ensure their survival. Anyone can judge her, but the truth is we were not in her shoes. As a mother, I can feel how her heart must have bled.

In a strange turn of events, your daughter herself has become a single mother too. Even with all the support I have been very fortunate to receive from you and Mama, it is still not easy to raise two children. I guess it is true that what does not kill us makes us stronger.

Indeed, these past four years have made me stronger, a heavy trial with my divorce. I know it must have been very hard on you too. It must have shattered all your ideals for a conservative family. I know you worried about what people might think (although I do not), perhaps worried for my future and happiness.

My ex-husband had manipulatively called our relationship a "marriage of three": Me-him-you. In truth, it was really you trying to help us out with our doomed-from-the-start marriage in any way you could (I do not think we would have lasted half as long without you). Our family had followed a strict Catholic Indo-Chinese checklist of who to marry. And look what happened – we had found The One. But the *Wrong* One.

His biggest loss, though, was you, because you are the best father-in-law any man could ever have asked for. I am amazed you are not jaded, even after so much betrayal, and you have welcomed, with so much warmth and love still, my new other half (a much-improved specimen, inside and outside). I guess it is a trait I have been fortunate to inherit from you. We are both not the sort who get jaded easily.

Perhaps it has always been you and me against the world. My relationship with you can be summed up as such: Imagine a cheerful lion cub, seen squarely straight from its front. And behind it – over it – a fully-grown lion, the leader of the pride. Its eyes pierce threateningly into ours (in contrast with his cub's), hovering above her, ready to pounce should anyone dare to attack his little cub. Though the cub may not always be aware of it, his presence is keenly felt.

That is how I have often pictured you.

It can only come from a loving and protective father, and I carry it with me like an invisible shield. You might have been very strict with me as I was growing up, but I never once doubted your love. I know I *am* important and of value. When push comes to shove, you are always there.

Remember when I had that fight with that boy in Primary 4? You turned up in school the next day and raised hell. The truth was it was actually *me* who smacked him first!

I also remember when we had to make our dramatic escape to the airport in that wretched year, 1998, after the fall of President Suharto. A turbulent time it was. During that perilous ride, we were in danger of encountering the mob. But I knew if it came towards us, you would hold them back as best you could and if need be, sacrifice your life to let your family run off to safety. You showed me what a man should be.

I can see now your foresight in moving us to Singapore

when the time called for it. Many years you had prepared for it. People called you the boy who cried wolf, always erring on the safe side. "Why all these precautions for the apocalypse?" they had laughed.

But guess who had the last laugh? You were proven right.

It was not easy for our family, having to uproot to another country like that, leaving all we had behind. Each of us struggled in our own way. You sourced and procured everything and supported us. From finding a home, to a car, and your adventures in securing a school for both my brother and me. Until today, you still support me and your two grandchildren. I will tell them all you have done for them. No father and grandfather could be more generous.

Thank you, Pa, for the childhood you had given me. I remember you brought me to the badminton hall every Saturday; I was more interested in the jungle surrounding it rather than the badminton itself. I remember those road trips too. And all our travels overseas. I have always loved Singapore, in particular because you took us there on a regular basis. Memories of soccer, badminton, boxing, the search for the best sound system. My childhood experiences are rich and varied because of you.

Not only that, you had also planned and trained me well from a very early age, bought all those encyclopaedias when I first learned to read. English is not my first language, yet I have now become a writer. This is as much your success as a parent, as much as mine.

Above all, thank you for killing all those cockroaches and chasing away rats! Thank you for accompanying little me in the dark of the night to the toilet, when you yourself must have desperately needed sleep. My father, the hero. They do not make men like you anymore these days.

And thank you for my dogs. Mama hates dogs but you could not stand me crying over dead dogs, so you always bought a new one for me. We do not just have our shared love of German shepherds, which divided our house into two camps. Whenever I did something that annoyed her, Mama used to mutter under her breath: "Just like her father." My brother, too, often said cheekily that he could guess who was walking outside his room by the sound of my footsteps, which was so much like yours, except they were lighter and smaller.

In recent years, whenever we have our little arguments, I try to look into myself, to observe my own mechanism as a way to understand you better. Now that I am a parent myself, I also realise that parenting is something we all learn on the job. As parents, we can only do the best we can under the circumstances and by the example we set. So, Pa, whatever disciplinary methods I had once found too tough or disagreeable, I can say now that I have forgiven you and understood you better.

Yes, I know we do not always see eye to eye. I am sorry if I were a disappointment. I was not born a boy, I could not run your factory; I sucked at badminton. I liked to go home late. Bloody hell, I am divorced, and certainly a pioneer in that department in our extended family – on both sides. I sure hope nobody else will follow suit.

I am sorry if it is hard for you to be my father.

I am sorry I could not fulfil your traditional views of what a lady should be. I have always lived life outside the box. I am not conservative. I often challenge and disagree with you. I am costing you a lot. But Pa, I hope you know I try to make you proud of me in my own way and until the end, I will look after you. I hope one day I will have the chance to prove myself on this.

Thank you for being so faithful to Mama. You never, not even once, behaved in any questionable manner towards other women. Not the slightest bit. Even in her older years, I know you still see her as that leggy girl in a miniskirt whom you first saw when she was 19.

Here is a man who says that "my wife's place is by my side", not as a housekeeping aide. For you, cooking and cleaning you can pay for, but your wife is irreplaceable. You love exchanging ideas with her, you appreciate her input in your business decisions. Whenever you have to travel alone, you try to minimise the time away from home.

Oh yes, of course, there are fights – I have heard you two. And your funny old folks' bickering today, like if the car window should be opened or closed, whenever you drive her around. But in any disagreement with the outside world, even with Mama's family, you always back her up – 101 per cent. "Right or wrong, she is my wife," you would say. It can be a little indulgent, but it is beautiful for a child to see.

For a man who grew up without a male role model to look up to, what a feat.

Finally, if I may, my humble two cents' worth from a child to her father:

Learn new ways to have fun. Put aside fear, accept that some things you cannot change. Enjoy your grandchildren and friends. Enjoy life.

I wish you to live long and enjoy your golden years to the full. You like to tell me that 90 per cent of the things we worry about will not happen. Pa, perhaps it is time for you to walk the talk. Trying to control people and circumstances outside our control is like holding sand in our fist; it will slip through our fingers. Also, come to terms that we have to go on living with this coronavirus somehow, peacefully, and not stress ourselves and people around us.

Christina with her father.

You have achieved more than what most people can say in their lifetime. You have been greatly blessed. In the end, it is our Maker who decides, how long, where and when.

Epilogue:

After many years of life at the orphanage, the little boy decided to run off and find his Mum. He worked odd jobs, sometimes sleeping on the streets, but he continued studying. He took night classes, made it as an auditor, lecturer, and businessman. That leggy, pretty girl, he was asked to tutor by his colleague, became his wife.

In his golden years, he has two MBAs gracing his wall, a testament of the value of education which he continually advocates. He lives happily in Singapore with his wife, children and grandchildren. He mentors the youth, sings in the choir, and continues to help others anonymously. Not too shabby for a little orphan boy, I would say.

Here is to more decades of our father-daughter adventures. I love you, Pa!

Your loving daughter,
Tina
Jan 20, 2021

Christina Thé is the author of two bestselling humour books, *Diary of a Former Covidiot* and *Misadventures of a Little Soprano*. As a soprano, she trained at London's Royal Academy of Music and has enjoyed singing at the Carnegie Hall. Amongst highlights of her operatic career was performing Queen of the Night in *The Magic Flute* at the National Opera Center in New York. Christina regularly appears in Singapore's opera scene and writes humorous realistic fiction while leading life as a modern single mother.

My Father, Inspiration of My Life

Louis Tong

Dear Dad,

Happy 80th birthday! Today, as on every birthday, you will try to keep it low key. But I am grateful to have you in my life and, on this significant day, wish to relive some of our memorable times. In the album with this letter, you will see some old photographs of these moments.

Thanks for being a pillar of strength during my formative years. By encouraging me to work hard, you had helped me to harness my willpower to make my dreams come true. This is in keeping, of course, with your name, Chin Sye, which means "rise up like a lion" in Hokkien. And you often said these words whenever my morale was low: "Son, I wish I have had the same opportunities as you do. If I had a second chance, I would put up a fight." I could still remember your appearance as you said this — jet-black hair falling into your eyes and thick, round, Harry Potter glasses (before they became known as such).

In fact, over the years, you had shared some precious experiences with me and demonstrated the skills required to deal with difficult situations. For instance, the photograph of me smiling in front of the Delta Swimming Complex was taken after my 10th birthday when Mother had signed me up for swimming lessons.

But the coach's lesson plan for me was literally to sink or swim: "If you dunk your head in the water enough times," he had said in a gruff voice, "you will be able to swim."

Your approach was kinder. You said: "Do not be afraid of the water." Then you showed me how to take regular breaths, reassuring me that with my lungs full of air, my body was naturally buoyant. To prove your point, you would lie supine in the water, keeping still with your body straight. "You can use the floating board till you are convinced," you added.

After much practice, I got rid of anxiety and did not have to use the board anymore. In fact, I loved swimming so much that in the early mornings, before a soul appeared at the Raffles Institution pool, I would hop into the blue water. My head, as if belonging to a dolphin, would dip in and out of the calm water.

You also taught me the skill of catching fish with a cast net. Wading into the water, you demonstrated how to open and throw the net wide, and close it afterwards. I looked at the heavy sinker weights at the rim of the net and thought: Not so fun doing this.

"It is not about brute strength," you said. "See, you can do it like a pro after a few times."

We did not always catch tonnes of fish, though cleaning up took time. While the sky continued to darken, I would never forget the mud and dampness in my swimming trunks, the boredom of waiting for wet sand to dry and flake off from my body.

Another precious memory was rowing out to sea in a tiny raft in Marina South, which was being reclaimed at that time. This trip was amazing, partly because of the location. Here, the proud Marina Bay Sands would one day be built. You called that fun — two grown men sharing a toy-size boat. But I found it hilarious, because when we sat facing each other, our legs protruded out of the edge of the vessel. After we rowed out far enough in the open sea, to my horror, you started to let the air out of the raft.

This must be some kind of commando training, I thought.

"What are you doing, Dad?" I said, trembling, though, by then, I could swim competently.

"Fear not," you reassured me. "Look, much of the air has gone now, right? But we are still floating. Why? Because it is hard to release all the air." We even tried to re-inflate the raft a little, blowing into it while treading water.

Trust you to incorporate survival training on these outings! From this, I learned the benefits of being calm and rational, and the need for rehearsing emergency responses. Your advice has actually helped me tide over obstacles in life. For instance, I stayed positive even after receiving news that my research projects might be disrupted because all my staff had gone on maternity leave.

However, your enthusiasm in my favourite hobbies did not always go down well. When I wanted to play football, you bought me "proper" boots and rather *atas* knee-length socks. Not cool, Dad!

"*Oi, hao lian* (show-off). This is not the Manchester United football club," one of the boys said.

The *kakis* in my neighbourhood played football in their slippers and grimy, see-through t-shirts, so they did not fancy being outclassed by someone wearing professional gear.

"Oh yeah? Is this Liverpool?" As a child, I knew only two other English football clubs. But I was not sure how to say "Arsenal" without sounding indecent, so I settled for Liverpool instead!

Forgive their teasing, I told myself; they were probably more jealous of me than anything else. But the pressure was on. I had to play as well as I dressed.

Dad, you did too much that time. The soccer shoes almost ruined my plan, which was to blend in with the boys, not to become a solo star. Thankfully, they accepted me in their team.

***

In two of the photographs, I wore the white uniform of Raffles Institution. You seemed disappointed when I chose to go there for my secondary school education. Why did I not choose River Valley High School, well-known for teaching Chinese at a higher level? I had opted for Raffles, not only because it was the premium school, but also because its student population was cosmopolitan and diverse.

Did you have something against English schools, or just the idea of learning the English language? At the same time, you told me that since I was proficient in English and comfortable with word processing software, you requested that I type your consignment letters to the art galleries. Eventually, did you accept that English literacy was critical in a globalised world? Did you confuse speaking English with being an Anglophile? I knew you disliked the British because they had surrendered Singapore to the Japanese without putting up a real fight. But, Dad, speaking English, reading English poetry and watching English plays do not make me loyal to Her Majesty, the Queen of England!

Though you are proud of your Chinese heritage, I notice that in another photograph, our family had dinner with two visitors seated at the table — an Indian man and a middle-aged Caucasian lady with curly hair that reached her shoulders. This scene clearly portrayed the absence of any racial prejudice on your part. This might explain why I, too, appreciate diverse cultures and easily embrace a multiracial Singapore identity. In my own house, I have also invited people, especially foreign visitors, to stay as guests. I pray, even in the face of socially divisive situations, to always believe in a common humanity.

***

I have not known you to express your feelings — not even when I graduated from medical school, became a national science scholar, was conferred a PhD degree and awarded full-tenured professorship. I would have appreciated an outward sign of your pride in my achievements, but I came to understand that you were inherently reticent and stoic, so I had to be satisfied with seeing only the glow in your eyes.

In childhood, I would sometimes encounter your rage. After an unsound investment, you suffered financially and declared bankruptcy, preventing you from travelling. That must have hit you hard. Was that why you became foul-tempered? Regardless of these difficulties, you went out of the way for me. This happened when I briefly worked in Sunderland as an adult. You flew 11,000km from Singapore, rode on two trains, turned up at this little-known place in Northeast England and said: "How is everything? There is *mee rebus* in the luggage."

***

Some of my favourite memories are about your work as an artist. Remember, Dad, how your wooden painting easels and brushes used to be all over our living room? Did you ever realise that even after the oil paints had dried up, I still could not resist running my fingers over the canvas? I loved feeling the coarse ridges and valleys of your paint strokes. So glad you did not tell me off.

If you remember, the unforgettable smell of solvents often suffused our three-room HDB flat. Did you pour turpentine to make the oil paints more fluid? I did not know then, that the fumes were, in fact, hazardous. At that time in Singapore, glue sniffing was a social problem among teens. Just imagine: I could have grown up in a constant state of intoxication from inhaling the fumes all those years ago! Or perhaps I could have even sustained brain damage! I would giggle at this memory years later during my training in medical school. But seriously, Dad: Did you consider using almond oils? At least the vapour would have been more tolerable.

In retrospect, I can see what a unique childhood you had given me. You were a painter, artist, graphic designer, art instructor and lecturer. In my school, nobody else's Dad had that colourful a career. When asked to describe your job, I would wink, as if letting on that you were a secret agent, spy, investigator, whistle-blower and adventurer all rolled into one.

In the early 70s, your paintings depicted commercial barges and river boats that once lined the busy Singapore River. You also painted traditional Chinatown shophouses, coolies and *samsui* women. When I look at these dusty paintings now, old Singapore seems to speak a thousand words, of the price we had to pay in becoming a metropolis. At the same time, your paintings also taught me the importance of documenting things for posterity. Later, in my scientific career, I would apply the same meticulous discipline of observation, recording and even storytelling, treating data as snapshots of "truth" captured in specific moments of our lives.

Another photograph that brought back memories was about a school project: Designing a logo on the theme of saving water. My jaw dropped when you produced the airbrush. My heart almost stopped when you switched on the air compressor to power the spray. The thunderous noise, reverberating in our tiny HDB flat on the 5th floor, with those wafer-thin walls, ceiling and floor!

Since we had to keep the main door open to allow ventilation, locking only the metallic gate, passers-by could see our "misdeeds". "Mum, there are a few people outside. They seem a little unhappy," I shouted above the deafening roar.

"Are you folks using a pneumatic drill?" one of the visitors asked, covering his ears.

If I did not respond, they would have called the Singapore Civil Defence Force, which had just been formed that year

(1982). "Calm down, fellows. The building is not going to collapse. The HDB engineers took this into consideration when they built the flat." Okay, that was not what I actually said. Instead, I had told them, with an uplifted chin: "That is my art assignment. Want to try it?"

The secret of the airbrushing, you shouted to me, was the intense pressure. Without it, we would not get the colour so even. This effort, guided by you, won me a district-level poster competition. The concept submitted was a single, glorified drop of aqua blue water. After that project, I took my hat off to graphic designers. No design is ever too simple to execute.

Old Mr Phua, who lived on the floor above us in those days, came for a medical consultation yesterday. We had a good laugh again about that airbrush incident when he thought you were drilling a hole through the ceiling without the HDB's permission.

***

Even today, when I look at the postcard you had sent from Kathmandu, images of the travelling artist would appear. You carried the drawing frame like a wooden cross all over the globe. If sketching was not possible on location, you took pictures and made paintings from these images after returning to Singapore.

"What happened in Kathmandu?" Mum asked, after one of your trips. "You disappeared and we did not hear from you for two days!"

"What can I do? They declared a state of emergency and blocked the route to the airport," you said. That was in 2005, the year of Nepal's royal coup,

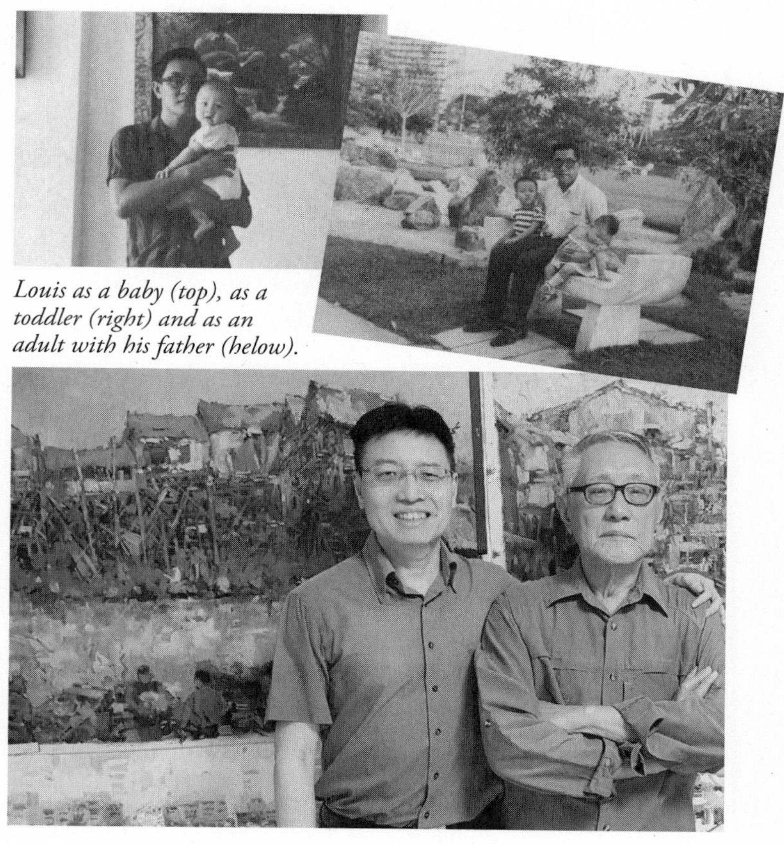

Louis as a baby (top), as a toddler (right) and as an adult with his father (below).

You fearlessly trotted off the beaten track, proud that you did not need tour agencies. Travelling on rugged routes, you chose to stay in hostels for backpackers, and places considered "more authentic" than the major business hotels. This was before the era of Airbnb and Google Maps. I imagined how you must have avoided the road blocks in Nepal, with compass and map in your pocket, hitched your rides from burly truck drivers, lugging the small electric rice cooker and the foldable easel stand.

Guess what, I have inherited that spirit of adventure from you. In my childhood, I explored weird smells and odd tactile sensations; in my scientific research, I was willing to explore any idea, no matter how bizarre, as long as it stood for something meaningful.

When travelling to conferences, I always desire to experience authentic cultures — hence, my fondness for the underground train to Yokohama frequented by the Japanese, rather than the luxurious airport coaches.

I was relieved that you did not push me towards any specific career. As an artist, you spoke highly of and with respect for scientists and physicians. Though I like scientific stuff, your work has given me a glimpse into the joy of creativity and artistic expression. As a physician, I have pursued innovative medicine because we have often been satisfied to provide only symptom relief and not directly address the problems faced by the sick.

Dad, I would not be where I am today without your wisdom, support and guidance. When mentoring students, I try to pass on this goodwill, guiding and helping them, as a father would. I am now in my 50s and hope it is not too late to say this: You have truly been my inspiration. I thank you now. And again.

Always,
Louis

Louis Tong, husband and father of two, is an ophthalmologist and professor at Duke-NUS Medical School. Associate editor of three international scientific journals, he has published short prose in *Twist and Twain*, *Active Muse*, *Yours2read* and *Cafelit*, and completed a short course in fiction writing at LASALLE College of the Arts. An active member of writing critique groups such as Singapore Writers Group, Caferati and Scribophile.com, he has completed a novel which was workshopped with these groups.

Berat Mulut: You will Always be a Part of Me

Alvin Tan

Dearest Pa,

The first description of you I can recall, till today, is Mummy's. She used to call you *berat mulut* which, translated from Malay, means "heavy mouth", referring to one being non-communicative. You were always not speaking your mind, you were always Mr Nice Guy and thus, always bullied at work. You would vent your frustrations only to Mummy at home.

But this trait of yours got me depressed when I was 14, thinking you were not an ideal father. I had wanted a father who would talk to me about life's challenges, ask me what was wrong when I was down. I wanted you to be the enabler and beholder of my strengths, to encourage and affirm me when I failed. Or simply buy me a tennis racquet and bring me to the court to let off steam.

I had thought then: I could get new friends, but how do I get a new Pa?

Luckily, I realised that my desire for this type of father came from a steady diet of American sitcoms such as *Father Knows Best, Family Affair, Bewitched, The Andy Griffith Show* etc. So, I began to dissociate the father image portrayed in such shows from the reality of you. I realised you love me in your own way. And once I saw and appreciated you for who you are and not through an American pop culture lens, my depression lifted soon after.

In your *berat mulut* way, you had always been supportive of me, in whatever I took an interest, as far as I can remember. When I had difficulties with Math in secondary school, you would ask if I needed tuition. I knew at that time it was challenging for us to afford a tuition teacher with your clerk's pay. But I was also conflicted because I had grown up in a bungalow in Siglap and we later moved to a terrace house in Telok Kurau. So, were we rich or struggling? It took me some time to understand that although we were living in a comfortable home, the wealth was, in fact, inherited and did not come from your hard-earned salary. Still, I knew it would be good for my future if I did not fail Math, so I decided to sign up for the tuition lessons anyway and stop feeling guilty about it.

There was also a time when the family income was not enough to provide for three children all schooling at the same time. Mummy wanted to work but you were concerned about her welfare, juggling work and housekeeping. So, you came to a compromise: If she could find a job near our home, you would be all right with it. That was how she ended up as a cook in the hospital just opposite our house. That worked out fine and the problem was settled for a good few years.

You also had no qualms about stepping up to do housework, be it sweeping the floor, bringing in the laundry, or buying groceries from the supermarket. I grew up watching you do these chores with no complaints. Although you might be *berat mulut*, you were also about putting love into action. So, I grew up believing very much in how to show love through my behaviour.

When you found it too expensive to maintain your car and wanted to sell it off, Grandma sulked about not being chauffeured to her sister's house on Sundays. At that time, you also used to drive us to weekend gatherings organised by Mummy's side of the family. Grandma complained: "What would people say and how would they view us if we did not own a car?"

In your quiet way, you dealt with the problem. You might complain under your breath, but you tried your best to reduce the conflict. From watching you negotiate and problem-solve, I learned the life skills I could never have in school.

From you, I learned that duty is a higher form of love. For instance, I recall there was once you received a call from your mother's sister. She was complaining about not being invited to the wedding of Anissa (your daughter). You explained that Anissa just wanted a small celebration with only immediate family members. Grandaunt retorted: "So if your daughter asks you to eat shit, you will? If she asks you to jump down from a block of flats, you will?" After ending the call, you looked at us and said: "One less house to visit next Chinese New Year."

You defended Anissa and made a choice to cut ties with Grandaunt because you would not want to live under such intimidation. But you did not let your ego rule over you; so you did not confront Grandaunt on the phone to have the last say. Through this, you showed me how to stand up for your loved ones.

You are unfailing in your duty to family, even when you had a problematic relationship with your demanding Mother, my Grandmother. I recall you had to drive her to her sister's house every Sunday. You had to make time for this, even though you must be tired from the work week and had your own family to take care of.

You keep faith with all who are important in your life, despite the ills they might have brought, intentional or otherwise. For instance, when your sister, my Mako, got into an accident while driving your car, you made some noise, but you quickly forgave her.

I have never heard you once complain about not having grandchildren. That the family name will not carry on. I recall your calm face as you looked into the coffin of Anissa, your daughter who had passed away from leukaemia at 30. I saw and felt your strength in that face, not hard or stoic, but graciously accepting what life brings to your plate.

Two years ago, when Alex, your second son, passed on, I could not find it in my heart to tell you as you were weak and fragile, always lying in your bed. I did not want to shock you in any way, so Mummy and I decided to hold the wake at the church and the funeral away from our home.

We never knew if you knew.

A few days after the funeral, I came into your room and you held my hands and shook them up and down, as if playfully. I recall you doing this with Alex when he was alive. I wondered if you had conflated Alex and me.

Pa, I am sorry I had behaved cowardly. But I was not ready for you to leave us yet. I am sorry I could not find it in me to tell you the truth.

Mummy made an altar with Anissa's and Alex's photographs next to a picture of Mother Mary. Every day, after praying at the main altar, both of you would go to the new altar she had put together and continue praying. Through this new ritual, perhaps you might somehow come to realise Alex's absence.

I used to regard those who perform rituals with contempt; I thought such obligatory gestures are empty, oppressive and hypocritical. Yet, every Chinese New Year and every birthday, I would get down on my knees to say to you and Mummy: "*Panjang, panjang umur.*" *Long life, long life.*

Even though Alex and Anissa had stopped doing this as they grew older, I have continued with it. I decided that since I do not hug you to show affection, this is a significant substitute and remains a meaningful practice to you and Mummy.

As I perform the ritual at least twice a year, I began reflecting if this greeting has been earned: Have I been a good son? Today, I value the lesson of how important duty is as a way of returning the love you have shown so generously and concretely to your children, especially in how you had brought us up.

For instance, I appreciate how you had always consulted me about matters and never insisted that I follow your recommendations. I recall that you valued freedom because it was not what you had from your Mother when you were growing up. So, you became the parent you wished you had.

And I saw that you had a quiet and peaceful relationship with your father. Ah Kong was a man of simplicity and, as far as I can recall, filled with equanimity. You, too, had that same calmness, even during a crisis. I am so glad I have inherited your forbearance.

In fact, I think I have also taken after your quiet, non-confrontational temper. Now, when I look back, I realise that the way I deal with authority figures has been inspired by your quiet riot strategy, which is not to react, but take time away from the heat of the moment so I can mull over the matter and respond later, without injuring anyone immediately or directly.

And true to your *berat mulut* nature, you and I have never really talked. From my aunts, I hear you used to love writing letters to them. In fact, you had written me lots of notes, mostly instructions and advice. I guess this was your attempt to reach out to me. I do reply, of course, but I address only the concerns you had written about. Of late, my notes ask after your health, if you are comfortable, tell you what the doctor has said, what time Mummy and the helper will visit you at the hospital, and such. Nothing more.

There are so many things to talk about, so many things you do not know about me. But what is essential is not talk, but that I am here with you today. And what I am today has been because of your unconditional love.

When you had your first major stroke, Mummy passed me your folder containing a list of things to do when you pass on. I was a little bewildered that you were so prepared, and had mixed feelings reading it. I still do.

Here's the list:

Alvin: Photostat about 10 copies of Death Certificate and inform the following -

1. CPF: So that they can divide the balance of my Medisave account to Mum, Alvin and Alex.
2. PUB: So that they can change the GIRO service to your account.
3. Property Tax: So that they can change the GIRO service to your account.

***

1. Fixed Deposit (OCBC): Joint account with Mum – no problem.
2. POSB - Also joint account with Mum – no problem.

***

See a lawyer to make a Joint Owners for this house later, so that you will have no problem in the future.

***

1. You can ask Mum to withdraw Fixed Deposit to settle my funeral bill.
2. Put my ashes in the sea and do not mourn too long.
3. I love you all and will miss all of you. Take care and goodbye.

Love,
Ronnie Tan

***

Pa, we may not know each other as deeply as we should as father and son. And yet, I hope you know that I love you and you will always be a part of me.

Alvin Tan is the Founder and Artistic Director of The Necessary Stage and a leading proponent of devising theatre in Singapore, having directed over 80 plays. He is also the current Artistic Director of the M1 Singapore Fringe Festival. Alvin has been awarded a Fulbright Scholarship, the Young Artist Award (1998) and the Cultural Medallion (2014). In 2010, Alvin was conferred the *Chevalier des Arts et des Lettres* by the French Ministry of Culture. The following year, he was awarded Best Director at *The Straits Times* Life Theatre Awards for *Model Citizens* by The Necessary Stage. He was also the Artistic Director of Peer Pleasure, an annual youth theatre festival by ArtsWok Collaborative (2015–2017).

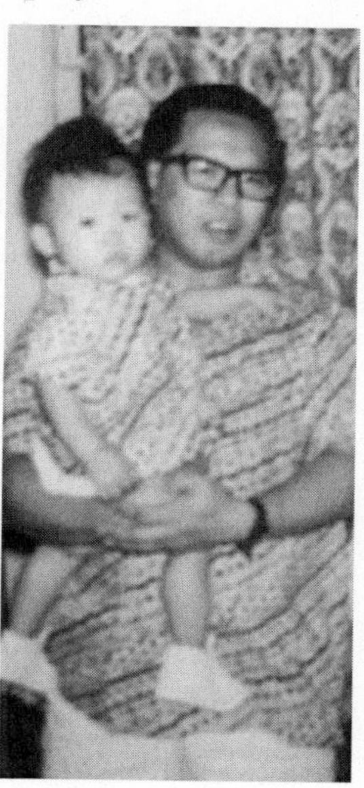

Alvin being carried by his dad.

Running the Good Race

David Kwee

> ...perhaps love, adopted a role called Being a Father so that his child would have something mythical and infinitely important: A Protector, who would keep a lid on all the chaotic and catastrophic possibilities of life.
>
> Tom Wolfe
>
> *The Bonfire of the Vanities*

Dear Dad,

This letter is to thank you for being the Dad whom we love. And for your inspirational example in how you have led your life.

You had a storied history as a sportsman and a doctor whom the community values. But most of all, you have been a good dad whom we have always looked up to.

Your early childhood years must have been precarious, because you were born in 1937 and would have been a young boy during the Japanese Occupation. Your family had to grow cassava and sweet potato to supplement irregular food supplies. Luckily, you had a strong, quiet influence in your father, Kwee Thiam Sioe, who was an ACS (Anglo-Chinese School) Housemaster and a church educator.

He was reliable and honest and thus, chosen as the first Asian Treasurer of the Methodist Church in Singapore and Malaya. Up till then, all treasurers had been American.

As Treasurer, he would have had to travel north to Peninsula Malaysia, cash in hand, to pay the various Methodist churches. You would have followed him on these trips and this developed his sense of trust in you as you served alongside him.

But it was not the safest of journeys then. On one trip, a Nigerian soldier, who was likely serving in Burma, was escorted on a trip to a sanatorium, still armed with his rifle. He went amok and shot up the railway carriage, resulting in six deaths and a few casualties. You dived to the floorboards and survived. The next day, *The Straits Times* had you on its front page describing the event.

Another trait you have is stoicism. Part of it stemmed from seeing how your mother had to juggle between being a nurse, working at the Jin Rickshaw building located far away in Tanjong Pagar, and being a mother, providing for five children. For breakfast, she would prepare the same food every day: Quaker oats, a can of condensed milk and five eggs for five children, all stirred up in a pot. It never varied. Lunch was also prepared at dawn and was later eaten cold by the children.

In school, though, you flourished. Not only did you do well academically, you were also a scouting leader. The late Senior Minister of State, Dr Tay Eng Soon, would mention to Mum that you were his Patrol Leader. The Scout's Oath – "To do your very best and to be prepared" – stayed with you as a life-long motto. I remember once that you had shown me your beautiful totemic cudgel that you had carved during your scouting days. It was most fascinating for a child to see.

In sports, you had a solid reputation. For several years, you were the ACS 100m and 400m champion. Mum still remembers your outstanding time of 11.4 seconds for the 100m. And you anchored the ACS team to clinch the interschool Sir Arthur Young 4x100m Cup and the Tan Siang Hoon 4x400m Cup. In fact, after the Tan Hoon Siang Trophy was won three times, ACS got to keep the cup permanently and it was proudly displayed in the school. To me, those black-and-white pictures of you in your athletic shirt, with the prominent ACS crest, are most precious.

You had told me you were glad for sports, for that was how you had met Mum. She saw you for the first time at the RGS (Raffles Girls' School) track and field meet, which had an invitational inter-school 4x100m relay. You had already known who she was because Mum, after being runner-up for several years, was a top girl in RGS.

Later, in medical school, the two of you became classmates and were soon inseparable. In the university, she was a pageant queen. Her other talents included playing the piano for church. You were married in 1963 and I look fondly nowadays at the black-and-white photos of that special day, with you in horn-rimmed glasses, and Mum in her wedding dress. Both of you looked so radiant. We three children were born in the next few years. You and Mum managed to balance work with bringing us up.

As a doctor, you were serious and focussed in your pursuit. You had, for a while, ophthalmological training. You had a steady pair of hands and could have done delicate eye surgery. But general practice became a calling and was a better job too, as you were starting a family and needed to spend more time with your children. You sourced a suitable location for a clinic and, with a loan from both sides of the family, bought a shophouse in Bukit Timah near an ever-flooding canal.

You would go on to spend the next 32 years at the practice. It operated morning, afternoon and night. People could even set their clock by your punctuality. You built it up from the first day, starting with a single patient, to a busy practice, seeing all conditions across all ages. It was meaningful work, because you sometimes ended up looking after three generations of family members, from babies in cradles to the elderly. Bukit Timah was more rustic back then; there were still several kampongs around the neighbourhood. Your bazaar Malay was good and all your patients, from senior civil servants to paupers, were treated at affordable rates. You are an old-world gentleman and thus, what endeared you to your patients was your steady approach, sensible prescribing, and connecting with them in your succinct and comforting manner.

For the first few years, we were living on the second floor of the shophouse, above your clinic. In the 60s and 70s, life was simple and we were happy and contented. Traffic was always whizzing by outside, so our childhood was cloistered in fairly small rooms and a sitting room. At that time, youngest brother Alex had not been born yet. Sister Elaine and I had the simple pleasures of basic toys, sitting around the living room with the TV set on, and old faithful *amah* Ah Cheong not allowing us to venture past the child gate put up before the stairs. I remember you, Dad, dressed in a singlet and sarong, being entertained by my baby language as I pointed to various objects. For some reason, I had found your cigarettes tempting.

I remember there was once an anti-smoking campaign on TV, which showed a skull next to the smoker. One day, Sis and I cried that we did not want to see you die. Promptly, you went cold turkey and quit. Just like that.

There would be great excitement during the yearly floods, which would reach the top floor of the clinic, sometimes depositing fish. I recall, Dad, that once, you had jumped into the deep waters, fully clothed, to rescue a child who had fallen in. In the process, you had lost your glasses but you did not mind it.

After a few years, when you and Mum had saved enough, we moved to a more comfortable house.

Growing up, we had probably grown fat on parental love and feeding, especially the Tuesday $1 Coney dogs from the longhouse-shaped A&W on Dunearn Road, plus root beer served in frosty mugs. We would also visit the American diner-like Magnolia Snack Bar on Stamford Road, with its booths, shiny straw dispensers and Magnolia ice-cream. The Silver Spoon at Supreme House had good set lunches. Other times, after a hard day's work, you and Mum might indulge us in a night snack in the best hotels, such as The Shangri-La or Hotel Malaysia. In those days, Koek Lane would be lined with pushcarts selling hawker food delights – we would sometimes end up there for supper.

Despite giving us these treats, you and Mum would sometimes ask us: "Have we spent enough time with you?" For us, it was an unnecessary question. We knew the two of you were working hard; we were also blessed with a network of grandparents, grandaunts and other relatives who shared in the caregiving.

The more relevant question, as I look back on your life, is: What are the lessons that you had imparted to us?

Maintain a sporting life (never too late to start golf!)

Mum joined you, after you had run the clinic for many years as a solo practice, and it finally gave you a bit of a breather. That was when you took up golf, at the relatively late age of 40, and you worked hard at the game, four days a week on the course, and three days at the gym.

I remember you practising diligently with hundreds of balls at the range, and also in our garden with plastic balls. It was not the easiest of games but you kept at it. In fact, you had an amazing run of three-holes-in-ones when you were already a grandfather. The result: Three lovely porcelain plates on the dining sideboard, given by the club, to commemorate your achievement.

Valuing travel

Our family travels started early, with numerous road trips up north to Malaysia. Our first big overseas trip was when we were aged 10 or 11. That was when we could get cheaper airfare for children under 12. Armed with Arthur Frommer's guide, *Europe on $5 and $10 a Day*, we explored Europe, not on palatial 1st class train, but on 2nd class Eurail with the occasional hard board for seats. We ate packed sandwiches and slept on overnight train coaches at times. Before we left, you explained the trip was a sacrifice in clinic earnings and airfares were expensive. But it was important for us to learn new perspectives in life through travel.

Indeed, the memories and impressions were indelible. As a result, we had no hesitancy, during our undergraduate years abroad, to do our own travels. And you were not overly worried when I was backpacking alone across the US, or when Sister was in Beijing University during the Tiananmen demonstrations in 1989.

One of the most meaningful trips was when you sent me to St Andrews for my studies. You helped me lug a bag of warm clothes for the Scottish winter – and an anatomy skeleton. There, at the edge of West Sands, where they had filmed the famous run of the Oscar-winning film, *Chariots of Fire*, was the Royal and Ancient Clubhouse and the Old Course, which we treaded reverentially. We caught a game at a less famous golf course and then went on a whisky trail up north, near the quiet lochs. A few years later, we took another golf trip, this time to the Bali Handara, set in a memorable 4000-ft caldera. These were precious times together, Dad – just you and me – and much treasured.

Be a bedrock of stability for your kids

Dad, I am amazed you could often leave your work stress behind and enter your home with an unburdened heart. It is difficult to do so nowadays.

Not only did you leave your stress behind, you had also never placed any stress on us by insisting on good academic results. To a child's developing brain, feelings of self-worth, love and acceptance by a parent are important. These you had given us unreservedly.

Even when one of us experienced a failure, you did not remind us of it or harp on it. In our eyes, we saw you and Mum as helpers, not as watchdog, in our development. You appreciated your children for who they are, as unique individuals, and not because of their achievements. You believed the best in people.

Your grandchildren have also found in you a cheerful grandfather who had never failed to pick them up them on time from kindergarten and enjoy a good chat with them in the car.

Be responsible and reliable

In your approach to work, you were systematic in how things were settled every day and never left to fester. And you were conscientious, arriving at the clinic early so you could close it on time, mindful that the nurses had their own families to take care of and would want to leave work on time. This is why they are loyal, staying with us even after 30-odd years with the clinic.

And, of course, Dad, you were the best mentor anyone could have had, helping me navigate the intricacies of a GP practice when I joined you. As with your nature, you made sure the clinic was renovated and in the best state before you handed it over to me.

From young, whether being a good brother or a dutiful son, you have developed a character that people could trust. You were never pessimistic, always positive. You gave people encouragement, keeping fault-finding to a minimum so that, little by little, they grew steadily. Whether or not they were your family members, patients or friends, you were always gentle and courteous. The key to this consistency was in your character – stoic, uncomplaining, having only simple needs, grounded by faith in God.

You felt it was very important to grow spiritually. These last two decades had been inspirational, as I observe how you became a cell group leader, hard at work with the Bible, cultivating wisdom from your regular studies. Late in life, you learned a new skill, the difficult art of communal prayer. Not only that, you began donating more to charity and you supported Mum in her social concerns work in the church. As a result, I believe the family has been spiritually enriched and the most blessed sound we have heard, a few times a year, was your voice leading the extended family when they came over for reunions.

In this closing chapter of your life, I think you are at great peace. You have redefined success for yourself. You did not place emphasis on success or money. This last phase of life is about your health and well-being.

I truly thank you for the example you and Mum had set for us. You have always cared for each other tremendously, for better and worse, in sickness and in health. The time granted by God is short and precious. But you made sure to leave us a sound legacy. As we take our different paths in life, we know you were always there, being supportive.

We love you, Dad!

David Kwee is a family physician. He studied Medicine at the University of St Andrews and University of Manchester, where he developed a love for wind-swept vistas, museums and galleries, and celebratory malts. He loves running at interesting locales around the world, bringing his family to yurts and desert tents while in Singapore. He often tramps the trails with his wife, Bing Yin. They have two children, Christopher and Cheryl.

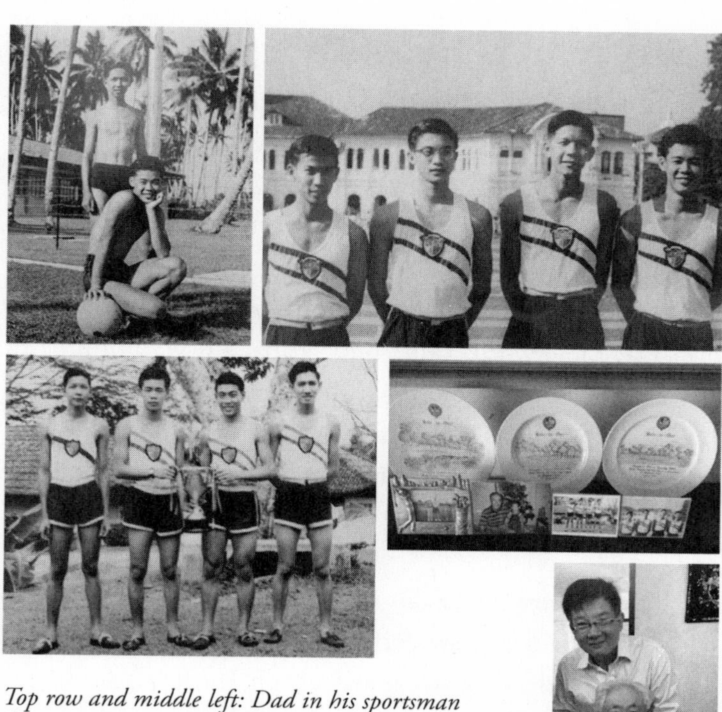

Top row and middle left: Dad in his sportsman days. Middle right: Three Hole-in-ones while golfing in his 60s. Bottom right: Dad and I.

Always the God-like Superman

Hoh Chung Shih

Remember that night when I said I could never be like you? I know it must have been a strange statement to make out of the blue. It was one of those nights when I was young and you came in to check if I was asleep. Though it was dark, I knew it was you. You bent over to take a closer look at me and at that moment, you realised I was looking back at you. You asked why I was still awake. Not knowing what got over me, these words came out: "Papa, I don't think I can be like you." Instead of being surprised, you simply smiled. I could not read your face if you were amused or curious. I guess not knowing where this sentiment came from, I felt like I was in a dream, and I think I quickly drifted back to sleep.

Why do I remember this scene?

I know these last few years have been really hard on you. The scolding, the regrets, the exhaustion, the fears, the blame, the whining, the rage – all these you have shown generously to everyone at home, family friends, even people at the hospital. I can only guess at the bigger storm and deeper turmoil seething inside you.

You have always appeared like a god-like superman to all of us. But now, you seem to have outgrown your body. It is tough to see how trapped you are in this body that does not quite suit nor serve you anymore. I am sure you must feel worse, especially when, for weeks, you do not know what the doctor might do to you next. Meanwhile, you just want to get it over and done with, in your usual efficient way, even as we try to ride out your surges of frustration.

Such strong emotions are hard-hitting, isn't it, although they are often fleeting, ineffable and effervescent like a fantasy. I am sure Mozart and Mahler would have understood you, since their music often deals with this intensity. But caught in your storm as your unwilling companions, we are slowly driven to exhaustion.

You have mentioned how your quality of life really matters and if you were paralysed, you would rather choose death. To enjoy life is all there is to it. But what is this enjoyment and what is life, really? It is true how we seek one nice distraction after another. But why do we do that? Maybe this active seeking gives us a sense of control, of free will, and as an expression of self-determination? Do we really enjoy such distractions as we seek and encounter them? Or have we simply gone numb, tired from the relentless seeking after so many decades, and realise that none of these distractions can really fill the void of unease within?

You are the one person who never fails to amaze everybody with your ever-changing distractions and range of interests. For example, I still remember vividly how we had started gardening – specifically, growing orchid plants. We would read orchid magazines (in Chinese, no less!) and hunt down really exotic breeds at all the most *ulu* farms at the far edges of this island. And then, we went into keeping an aquarium which, at the peak of our craze, had three huge tanks running with both fresh and saltwater fish!

Even now, in your 80s, you still continue to learn about and explore digital photography, along with being active on various social platforms, taking up courses and using SkillsFuture credits from the government. You even took up a series of baking courses that came with exams! Time just flew by as we got distracted, it seems!

But while we can enjoy life this way, with our endless pursuits, does it make the impending death more daunting, this perpetual postponement to face up to our own mortality? I can only guess at your fears as you lay there in bed, sustained only by various drips, waiting for weeks for treatment. You keep saying you have never felt so helpless. But we have always been helpless, no? Isn't being helpless our constant and common condition?

Whether you are aware of this or not, you have, in many ways, shown us our future. You have walked ahead, testing and trying life and its possible meanings. Your happiness and sadness, successes and failures, have become landmarks on this map of our lives. Your happy-go-lucky attitude is so lovable and intoxicating when situations are enjoyable. And you can always make something enjoyable.

You always could.

Always the god-like superman that you are; how can I ever be like you? One wise man once said you are my karmic lesson!

Hmm, I think his message is slowly sinking in. Through you, I see a probable path that awaits me.

But I had seen the dark clouds of this storm years ago. Perhaps you finally see what I saw then: The immense possibilities of life that make living almost impossible. The fragility of existence, coupled with the uncertain richness of every day, when the assurance of the body starts to give way with age, when *divertissements* of life start to run out. Where, then, is the superman? Who is the superman?

Mom seems to be the superman now. In her own quiet way, she has accompanied us all this way. Well, maybe to you, she is not quiet. She does rattle on at times, for sure, but I doubt we register or understand all that she says. We have witnessed how you both often talk to one another – or maybe talk *at* one another – with no sign of a reconciliation. Maybe all this charade-like communication is necessary for a family to stay together, at least in appearance... to get by?

Papa, how did you meet Mom? How did you know for sure she was the one for you? We have often heard your beautiful love story; how you were secondary school classmates who got married and eventually brought up a family of five, against the backdrop of our nation coming out of post-war poverty and turmoil, to where we are today, financially stable in a First World country. But how did you really meet, and why?

How can we see this latest act our family is playing out, to be a logical follow-up from such a magical journey? Mom has not changed, at least not to me. She is more predictable than before. Yet, you keep insisting that she has changed. So, if, as you have also insisted, you have not changed either, what has changed?

What has changed now is we have all grown old. Some of us, like Mom, have already accepted it as a fact, as well as the inevitable loss of control of our faculties. It seems Mom, with her less active pursuit of happiness, who does not need distractions to sustain her feeling of being alive, has a better grasp of real life as it unfolds.

Perhaps we should look to Mom, the woman you love and chose as your life companion. She has this way of just letting go, letting life present itself. When Superman becomes vulnerable under the effect of kryptonite, or when 007 is trapped or conned, or Don Giovanni is headed towards Hell – that is when the story begins to get interesting. So, shall we all ride this out together, and see what may come? I do not have to be like you, nor you be like Mom. We are wonderful the way we are as companions, as family, on this marvellous journey together, no?

I have always wondered what a family is. We definitely did not choose one another's company. But you did choose Mom, for sure. And Mom chose you. Do you remember the version of the story from your sisters, our aunts, about what your Mom had said to our Mom when she was first introduced to your family? What are we to make of that story, now that it is almost painful to be together?

My siblings and I must be quite a surprising bunch to you and Mom, coming one after another, adding to the crowd every three years, cluttering your 60sqm living space with noise and motion, complicating your relationship slowly but surely. Come to think of it, we have been together for more than half a century already! How time has warped around us five!

There is no sensible sequence or clear timing to any of these scenes in my memory that have surfaced, like the random pick-and-choose of movies at video rental stores, you letting us roam the aisles and raid the shelves for what we wanted to watch. We ended up bickering over the final selection, until you stepped in to convince us a 007 film would be the best choice of all. How true and wise you were at such moments. Those were rare moments when we came closest to attaining the Confucian ideal of a family: "君君臣臣父父子子". *Ruler be the ruler, subject will be subject, father, father, son, son.*

By this ideal, you are the husband, the father and the man of the family. But it was not easy being the father and the man of the household for more than half a century, right? Was it a stroke of precocious foresight that led to my curious question that night so many years ago? It just seemed so daunting a role to take up, or build up to, or carry on, when so little is within one's control. You, the man of the family, would understand better that life is without control or certainty.

Ah, I guess there is no one way to be in a life that presents and will present itself in such infinite, mysterious ways. So, let us just sit back and watch how this show unfolds, and be glad we are each other's audience. Maybe that is what 君君臣臣父父子子 really means. Regardless of differences, let us enjoy it while it lasts, for better for worse; it is just so many sparkles along the way flashing with fun, furies, fears and tears.

Papa, how long more will we have time together? Memories are like recurring dreams, and future fears linger like phantoms around the corner, waiting to pounce. Even the eternal present is fleeting. What remains is what each of us has to recognise within ourselves, and realise our song as we sing, sometimes harmonious, sometimes not; sometimes as accompaniment perhaps, changing keys, changing modes,

Chung Shih (right) with his parents.

changing meters, changing beat, but always flowing on together with time.

Thank you for being there and reflecting back on us as our realities, our journeys merged and co-emerged. Thank you for being our Papa as we continue to compose ourselves, our lives, our music.

Hoh Chung Shih is a composer and sound artist whose training in Western classical and contemporary music has led him to explore the intersections between the traditional and experimental, the avant garde and classical. His study of the quintessential Chinese literati musical practice of *guqin* (the Chinese seven-string zither) since the 90s led him to also appreciate Chinese brush, gardens, and ideas. Educated in Singapore as well as the US and UK, Chung Shih has wide interests in global cultures. His many interests include textile collecting, gardening and of course, travelling.

Birds Shall be Birds

Wong Ting Hway

Dear Dad,

I have been meaning to write this letter since we moved to our new home across the Pacific. The kids are laughing in the backyard, constructing a fortress from fallen branches and random rocks. They used to make fortresses in our old life too, from Lego, but I never paid it much attention.

Now, I am finally getting round to enjoying their creations. I am also setting aside time to record the lessons you have taught me – lessons I hope to pass on to my children one day. I am sending them to you to be sure that I have remembered the details correctly.

***

Before I left home for university, Sis asked what I thought of your lecture on "the birds and the bees".

What lecture, I asked, worried at what I might have missed out.

"The one where he tells you not to fall for the first guy who comes along, just because you are alone and lonely in a foreign land."

We both understood the implications. You and Mum had met while studying for your doctorates in the US, in an era when deserving foreigners could still get full scholarships.

It had always been a mystery to us how the two of you had ended up together, as different as you were.

Despite this, you never abandoned Mum, even when she requested and obtained a "friendly legal separation" after we grew up. A few years later, she conveniently forgot about the parting of ways when she began her decade-long journey through dementia, and you came back to care for her.

You shouldered a major part of the burden of her care. It could not have been an easy journey, neither as carer, nor as witness. We try not to imagine our lives like that – ending as husks of our past selves, lighting up only occasionally, when we recognise something or someone that ties us to our past.

Mum's dad and brother had also walked this journey, and Sis and I often wonder if that is our destiny too.

By then, I was married, and my husband got to witness and marvel at what you did.

You set the bar – high.

***

Whenever the kids are picky with their food, I would tell them about the Ethiopian famine that was all over the news when I was growing up in the 80s.

"Think of all the starving children in Africa," you used to say, whenever I failed to finish the food on my plate.

There was that one time I was flippant: "So, give it to them then."

You flew into a rage and to this day, I make sure I leave my plate clean.

What neither of us knew then, was that one day I would be working – in a different country, and a different war – where the children looked similar to those I had once seen on TV, their ribs sticking out, their bellies swollen.

I returned from a mission in Angola with Doctors Without Borders in 2002, just before the end of its civil war. But it was only after having children of my own, years later, cradling these plump babies, warm in my arms, that I began to understand what I had seen in Angola, and remember the sunken cheeks of the children who did not make it.

Maybe they sought help too late, maybe we lacked the right equipment, or maybe it was me, and my lack of experience. Now, when my children run up to me and hug me randomly, I remember the cries of those mothers who had lost their children, and I hold onto my own children a little longer.

It was also in Angola that I met the first man I ever brought home to meet you and Mum. After that introduction, I received my second "birds and bees" lecture from you.

While the first was about the decisions birds and bees make when alone and lonely, the second one warned against those that were old and inflexible.

According to you, there was nothing wrong with the patient and soft-spoken humanitarian worker I had brought home, apart from the fact that he was over 40 and had never been married.

"By age 40," you explained, "we men are set in our ways."

"Either his standards are too high – in which case, it would be a matter of time before he realises you are not perfect – or, he has a problem with commitment."

"Had he been married before, at least you would know that commitment is not an issue."

I never found out whether it was his race and not his age that had troubled you. I remember asking you some years earlier how you would feel if I married a non-Asian.

"Many things in life are like Death," you had ventured. "We will never know how we feel or what we will do until we come face to face with it."

A few years later, I brought Dan to meet you and Mum.

Fortunately, all went well, and we got married soon after, even though he was at the "stubborn old age" too. You never mentioned any concerns about him having unrealistic standards or a fear of commitment. Maybe he looked young.

By then, I myself was not that far from the "stubborn old age" either. It would be a few more years after marriage before I realised, it was a good thing Dan had never received a similar warning from his father.

***

When I found out I was expecting a boy, a friend congratulated me: "Great that the first is a boy, so your duty is out of the way."

I shrugged, nonplussed, as she added: "I was at your wedding; it is obvious you have married into a family with traditional Chinese values. No one would ever say it openly, of course, but it would definitely take the pressure off, now that you are having a son."

Dan's family wears its Chinese-ness on its sleeve, but so do you. Yet, growing up, I had never felt inferior as a girl.

I had to think hard to recall even one incident that hinted at any disappointment you might have felt in failing to perform your duty of having male offspring. Even then, it did not come directly from you, but an attribution from a woman who assumed she knew your every thought.

The first year that I topped my class, Mum had said: "Your father will be so proud. He wanted you to be a boy."

***

The third lecture you gave was different from the first two. I remember it as the "birds shall be birds and bees shall be bees" lecture.

As newly-weds, it was easy for Dan and I to agree to disagree. Married life was little different from our dating lives, except we no longer had to think about seating plans for the wedding or tiptoe around each other's parents.

Once the children came, minor differences of opinion escalated into major ideological divides that could change the course of human history (or, the children's future well-being, at the very least).

You pulled me aside one day after witnessing another one of our marital disagreements. I cannot recall what the argument was about – it might have been about the proper way of dealing with a picky eater.

Before her dementia, Mum took pride in being a fearsome Math teacher at work and an iron disciplinarian at home. We still speak of those times, when Sis and I were growing up, and she would insist that we all do something *exactly* her way, or refuse to let us engage in activities she deemed "a waste of time".

Her decisions might have been based on sound rationale, but with the hindsight of three decades, we would have likely turned out fine, with or without her heavy hand.

That streak of Mum's reappears in me once in a while. I like to pretend it is only with potentially life-threatening hazards (like an unsheathed penknife near the children's play-area). But in reality, it took me a while to learn to sit back and enjoy the journey.

You told me: "A couple can agree to disagree. Our children will not be ruined for life if they fail to acquire the super-power of keeping the floor crumb-free during meals (even if they are expected to leave a clean plate – every time)."

This became important when we had to uproot ourselves and move to Canada, Dan's birthplace, arriving just in time for the worst pandemic in a century. I was in an unfamiliar place with few friends and no job. A firm offer for part-time work in a remote part of the country had disappeared when many provinces locked down their borders to control the spread of the coronavirus.

For someone used to working long hours with no time to sit back and stare, that took some adjustment. With schools closed, the high point of each day was sitting at the dining table, teaching long subtraction (or something just as exciting) to two restless children.

I drifted around our new house. It was a while before I noticed it becoming a home, as Dan busied himself rectifying minor house defects and preparing increasingly ambitious meals, the aroma blanketing us as the sun went down.

One morning, waking up early out of habit, I remembered what you had once told me: "Sometimes, things do not turn out exactly as you had planned, and that is okay."

I looked around me, at the children slumbering in a mass of strewn bedlinen and stuffed animals, the moonlight through the window casting uneven shadows on the yet-to-be folded laundry.

We do not need to be in a constant hive of activity to be happy. Happiness is having a nest, defects and all.

Or a fortress of sticks and stones.

***

Last year, before we moved away, you planned a dinner for your nephew visiting from Texas. I had always known that you shared a deep bond with his father, your late second brother, who had supported you through your early university education.

I had not understood just how deep the debt was, until you told your story that evening.

Shortly after you were born in Malaya, just before the Second World War, your sister, the only girl in the family, died of illness. From your third-hand description, it sounded like whooping cough or pertussis. Grandmother's milk dried up from grief, so you were the only one among your siblings raised on milk powder.

After the war, the family could barely cope, and a decision was made to give one child away. The eldest could work to support the family, the second was old enough to help around the house, the youngest was Grandma's "baby". So, it was you, the third child, who was given to a poor childless carpenter from a small village. For a few months, you learned carpentry from your adopted father.

Dad, I always knew you grew up poor, but that was the first time I had heard this part of your life story. You were finally sharing this chapter, over a sumptuous meal in a restaurant that my daughter had happily labelled "very fancy". My cousin, immaculately dressed, headhunted several times in his career by multinational corporations, carried no trace of the poverty that his father, and mine, had been born into.

My rambunctious children may not notice this, for you are always the doting grandfather around them, but you have always been a man of few words. When you told your story that night, it struck me that that was possibly the longest I had ever heard you speak.

Listening to your voice under the soft lights, staring at the impeccable plating on the starched tablecloth in front of us, I wondered if your love of silence might have begun then, when your parents sent you to a small village to live with a lonely carpenter. It might also explain how a retired professor of chemistry possessed a craftsman's hands, ones that could restore broken items such that no one could guess where the original cracks had been.

A few weeks after you were given away, Granddad – your biological father – stopped speaking and eating. Eventually, your mother sent your eldest brother to bring you home. Granddad recovered immediately after you returned.

What became of your adopted father, I asked. After a few years, your letters to him went unanswered. And you never returned to the village.

At that time, schooling was delayed for most children

because of the war. On top of that, you began school later than everyone else in your class, unable to read or write.

It was Second Uncle who brought you up to speed, giving you lessons by candlelight late into the night. He was proud when you topped your class and years later, when you got a place at university, he supported your studies with his hard-earned meagre wages.

You became the first in your family, and the only one of your generation, to go to university. You went on to get one scholarship after another and eventually, a doctorate.

You told your nephew that after you received your first scholarship, you had returned the money to your brother, so that he could finally get married.

"Nine months later," you said and smiled at my cousin, "you were born!"

The kids were too busy with the exquisite food to hear that part of the story. If they had, they would have demanded an explanation – what did getting a scholarship have to do with my cousin being born?

And that would have meant a different lecture on the birds and the bees.

I have yet to find a name for this last lesson, delivered in an elegant restaurant, with Dan and the kids sitting next to me. But I am sure something will come to mind soon.

I do hope, though, that when the time comes for me to pass on your wisdom, they will understand: Their mother would not be who she is, without these lessons from you.

Love,
TH

Wong Ting Hway is a surgeon with research interests in healthcare inequality and frailty. In her previous life, she worked with Doctors without Borders and the International Committee of the Red Cross. When not walking around the hospital, she dances hip-hop with her children. Her poems and articles have been published in various anthologies, including *Dance the Guns to Silence* and *Medecins Sans Frontieres: Stories from the Field.* More recent essays, inspired by her journey with her mother's dementia, were published in *Grandmother's Garden.*

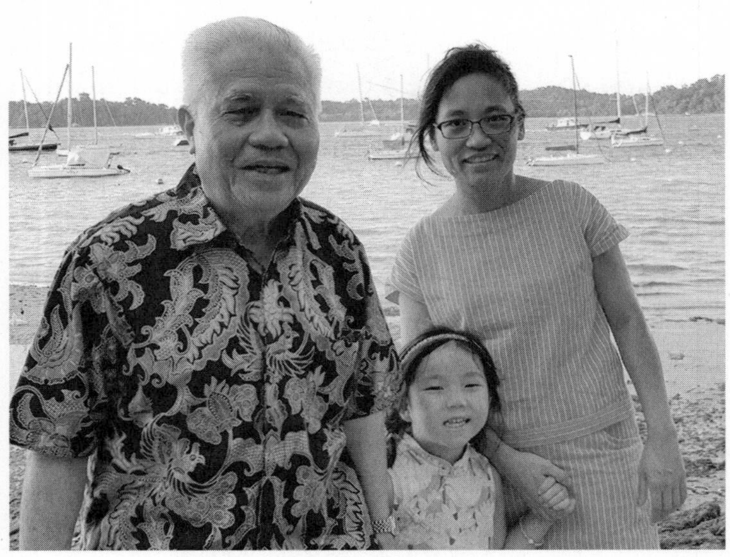

Ting Hway (right) with her father and daughter.

Life – As My Father Showed Me

Chee Soo Lian

Pa,

Nick dreamt of you again last night. Nick and Mee dream of you often, but I have only seen you twice in my dreams.

I think of you a lot though, especially when I have arguments with Mee. I wonder if she had often been the trigger of your hypertension, like how she would bring my blood pressure up. When you were alive, I had promised: "When one of you leaves, I will move home to be with the other." I meant what I said and after living out for 13 years, I returned back to our home after your death. Sadly, living with Mummy was not easy and I moved out again six years later.

I have no idea how you tolerated Mummy's stubborn nature, erratic moods and emotional play. For me, I have tried to believe the cause is the constant arthritic pain gnawing at her joints, or the insecurity stemming from the mother-and-daughter tension. Perhaps you understood something more – that at the core of Mee's existence is a deep longing to be constantly assured of our love, and she craved for our attention and time.

I used to think if she were to go before you, I would finally be able to spend more time with you and get to know you, like how a daughter wants to know her father more. With Mee around, however, there is no way each of us in the family can connect with each other, except through her. She has to be the centre that holds the family together and we can only be close to each other if she is assured that she is first in our lives.

The only time you would talk directly to me was when there were health issues. It was as if my knowledge of such matters had earned me the privilege. When you had water in your ears and asked me what you should do, we got a referral from Dr Lim and visited the ENT (ear, nose and throat) specialist together. In the doctor's chair, we both witnessed the scope going into your nasal passage and ear canal – you were thrilled that you could see your own anatomy so clearly. The doctor assured us that there was no growth and that he would just have to give you something to clear the passage. Over the weeks, the problem was resolved and there was still so much joy and excitement whenever you spoke about the scope and what you saw on the screen.

The most nerve-racking of these incidents was when you had a fish bone lodged in your throat. You and Mee were having your favourite *assam* fish head at Redhill when you thought you might have swallowed a fish bone. It must have been really uncomfortable, even though you did not choke on it. But Mee had decided it was no longer in your throat and your discomfort was psychosomatic. That afternoon, she had told you to simply "sleep it off and stop thinking about it"!

Honestly, I was horrified when you called and told me you had woken up and were quite sure the bone in your throat had not gone away. How could she have suggested something so ludicrous, putting your life in danger? I rushed to the flat and all three of us then got into a cab and headed for the A&E in the Singapore General Hospital. The X-rays confirmed it – you had a foreign object lodged beyond the back of your throat.

That evening, the whole family waited for hours near the operating theatre. The doctor said no surgery was necessary but the procedure of dislodging the bone was a delicate one and they had to put you under general anaesthesia. That night, I wondered if you were going to have a puncture in your throat or oesophagus during the process, and if that did happen, would we see you again?

The wait seemed eternal as your case was continuously delayed by the more life-threatening admissions in the A&E. When your turn finally came in the wee hours of the morning, a three-pronged fish bone was extracted. I remember rushing up to you as they wheeled you out of the surgical ward. Looking relieved, you held up a small Ziploc bag with the bone in it, smiling weakly and signalling to us that all was over and you had survived the ordeal.

You were not so lucky when you fell at home in November, 2013. You were no longer lucid after the bleeding had tunnelled into the deep recesses of your brain. You remained semi-conscious for two weeks; after which, we were informed that you had caught the MRSA (Methicillin-resistant Staphylococcus aureus) super bug in the hospital. As they wheeled you into the isolation ward, you were clearly anxious and agitated. You were not sure where you were being transferred to, even as I assured you that we were only arranging for you to be in a quieter ward. Later that evening, I sensed your agitation surrendering to resignation and perhaps, acceptance. You did not buy my lie and you knew the end was near. You were calm and at peace when we left the ward that night, and even when we saw you early the next day. But later that Sunday morning, you breathed your last.

***

Fathers are mostly seen in their capacity to provide for the family. I have heard about fathers who guided their children and fathers who abandoned their children, successful fathers and fathers who could not provide. I have never seen you in that way though. To me, you were simply the person you were, and you loved us. Between you and us, there was a simple karmic affinity – one of father and daughter, or grandfather and grandson. *Che*, Nick and I all identify with a part of you in us. Now, in my 50s, I see more and more of you in the person I have become. I recognise in myself the same lightness of existence I saw in you – not weighed down by the cares of this materialistic world, but buoyed up by infinite moments of simple joyousness in life.

Pa, you had a great sense of humour and you were always jovial. You allowed us access to many of the things you yourself enjoyed. I remember the family's weekend outings to the movies. You brought us to blockbusters like *Snake Man*, a popular Khmer film in the early 70s and the action-packed Shaolin films, including those set in the period of Emperors Yongzhen and Qianlong, with the terrifying mobile guillotines! Even when we visited your hometown, Taiping, we would frequent the cinemas. I remember catching a Tamil film about Lord Ganesh. We wept at the film's ending – only to discover when we returned to Grandpa's house that evening that I had a rash of bug bites on my buttocks.

This father-and-daughter love for movies carried on through my late teens and early 20s, when you and I would religiously watch Tamil films every Thursday night and Hong Kong blockbusters every Saturday. Our favourite were the slapstick black-and-white Tamil comedies with Nagesh, the king of comedy – a particularly skinny comedian whom you loved. I never knew if you really understood what you were watching because you did not seem to read the subtitles that ran too quickly. It was only after Mee's retirement, when she opened her convenience store and we heard you speaking to the Tamil workers, that we realised you understood some Tamil. We suspected your accent must have been rather off-putting, since the customers always looked rather annoyed when you spoke! You later explained that when you were helping out with Grandpa's fruit business in Taiping when you were growing up, you had mingled with Indian hawkers in the market and picked up some Tamil.

The other thing I enjoyed with you was exploring *ang moh jiak* (Western food)! In the afternoons after school, when I waited in the office where you and Mee worked, you would buy me my favourite Magnolia pyramid milk pack. It always came with the tip cut and a straw already inserted and you would watch your eight-year-old relish her packet of milk until the base of the straw made a scrapping noise in the empty packet. I remember how you would watch me drink – amused and totally satisfied that your child could enjoy such a luxury. Occasionally, you would ask to taste the milk and after one sip, you would chuckle and hand it back to me. When McDonald's opened in Singapore, you often bought me the fillet-o-fish after you realised I liked it at my first try. In-between these two experiences, we also had fries, sandwiches and at one time, even chicken chop!

Etched in my memory were also those bike rides on your Raleigh. At the end of a school day in St Matthew's Kindergarten, I would wait for you to ride by and put me on the rattan child-seat tied to the crossbar of your bicycle. I liked sitting astride the rattan seat, with your arms surrounding me, as you directed and steadied the handlebar. These bike rides continued during primary school. There were those mornings you and Mee discovered I had forgotten a textbook and she would make you fetch it to me. This happened frequently enough for some of my former classmates to recall how fortunate I was that my father was always sending me my books!

I went from the rattan chair to the crossbar and later, sitting side-saddle on the rear carrier when you rushed me to school on some mornings. One day, after I had heard you heave and pant going upslope, hurrying to get me to the school's back gate before the flag-raising ceremony, I knew that was the end of my bike rides. I told you: "Pa, I think cannot do this anymore... I have become too heavy for this bike." You smiled, and your expression betrayed how you must have felt – a mix of "duty done" and "my daughter's grown". There was a tinge of melancholy as I left you for class that morning.

What guided you in life was your love for your wife and children, your generosity towards the people around you and your free-spirited nature. Mummy, on the other hand, took on the role of the strong, long-suffering and dutiful wife, who supported her husband through those difficult years in the 60s to start a family and bring her daughters up well. Mee kept discipline in the house while you hardly scolded your daughters. I distinctly remember one night when I arrived home with a new haircut that was too short for any parent's liking. You were quieter than usual, then you walked over and coaxed me: "Next time, do not cut your hair so short *lah*." At that moment, I wished my hair would grow back the next morning.

Your gentleness extended beyond the family – you were always quick to help those in need and would place a few dollars in the hand of anyone crouched along the pedestrian walk, waiting for generosity from strangers. But you were not perfect, of course; we remember your quick and explosive temper, and your Hokkien swear words too! That did not matter to me though. What I learned from watching you was the importance of being self-assured, to be who we are – natural, unselfconscious, and refusing to be strapped by any code of behaviour expected of us.

Like you, I hardly care about society's expectations of me. In my early 30s, Mee's hopes for my future were dashed when I decided I had little interest in the accumulation of physical assets; I had also rejected the institution of marriage. Mee and I fought frequently and that brought you grief. During one argument, you insisted that I stopped my nonsense and listened to my mother. Your face reddened and I resented you for siding with her. That was one rare moment when I saw your exasperation at what I was doing. It dawned on me that if I had continued to defy Mummy, I might have just killed you with a heart attack. Your rage – a father's rage – put me in my place. That night, I saw you as Mee's husband, perhaps even more than you were my father. Much as Mummy appeared to be the more dominant spouse, you were very much the support and strength that had sustained her.

Mummy could get away with almost anything with you. You listened to her nagging and her unreasonable demands with humour. In fact, you indulged her even more as you aged. You did not like it when Mee was difficult, but you almost always chose not to react, unlike *Che* and me. You understood Mee the way we didn't. In the years before your death, whenever she and I got into our fierce fights, you would appeal to me to accept my mother like you did, in the way you had loved her and kept her going.

Years later, when you lay in hospital, half-conscious, I watched Mummy wrestle with her own guilt for lacking the confidence, strength and stamina to see you through your illness. In her fear and desperation, she kept saying that if we had to look after you, we would have grown to dread it. I detested this Hokkien idiom she kept repeating: "In prolonged periods of sickness, children turn unfilial." Why was she dragging *Che* and me down to her own personal struggle? When you passed away, she felt very much on her own, even though she knew she had Nick and us. I was petrified listening to her lament during your wake – her wailing in her eulogy revealed that your departure had left her like a child, and panicking, because she knew then that no other person was going to tolerate and stand by her the way you had done all those years.

In the two years following your death, I saw Mee work hard to come to terms with her decision (made with us) on not proceeding with surgery for you after your fall and stroke. Her grief was prolonged by her sense of guilt. Outwardly, though, all that grief was framed as sadness that came from both your love being indomitable and her loss. For a period of time, the grief and guilt consumed her. She lost a tremendous amount of weight and I often wondered if she was going to pull through. She did overcome the grief and recover eventually, but at each visit to the cemetery, she would still touch your tombstone lovingly and tear a little.

Mummy will be 83 this year and she mentions death often. A person in her 80s must wonder when her final day will be. I look at her fingers, bent and deformed from rheumatoid arthritis, and her worn soles stripping away her confidence in her physical balance – she now walks more cautiously. I ponder on her difficult adolescence after the war, following her father's suicide, which you would have known since you were acquainted with her family when you worked for their relative in a shop below them.

Soo Lian, aged 10 and her father.

Now that I have had a glimpse of her past, I have perhaps begun to understand why you were determined to make life easier for her by simply allowing her to have her way a little. It is still difficult for me to see reason in the things Mee says and does, but each time I am close to losing my temper, I think of her life and how you had chosen to be gentle with her. And that guides me, Pa, to be a little kinder to my mother.

Chee Soo Lian sees the need for us to listen to our parents' narratives of the past and record them. By delving into their past and ours, we can begin to thread together lives and events that have shaped our identity. Another path to understanding ourselves better is through travelling – visiting places with which we connect emotionally. Believing that she might have been a sojourner on the ancient Silk Road, she has visited numerous places in China, India, Pakistan, Iran and Turkey. When not seeing to such matters in life, she works as an editor and also teaches English to foreigners.

ΓΙΧ (Aleph Tav)*

Natalie Ng

Even after five years, nothing has changed about the hospital, Dad. The façade hasn't changed; the Toast Box outlet in the mall across the road, where I used to buy your breakfast, is still there. The same hospital where you had faded away peacefully after a shot of morphine; after which, they removed the tubes, cleaned and wrapped you in a shroud, and sent you off to the undertakers.

Did you feel like you were running out of time, Daddy? Maybe you knew, after all. That morning, right up till just before you became unconscious, you were still on your phone, calling your secretary, checking prices of business trades.

You had pulled me into your room and said: "When I go, I want you to take care of my finances." But I would not have any of it. As Christians, we believe God could turn the situation around 360 degrees and heal you. But I should have known better as I watched your condition deteriorate. Maybe I was in denial.

---

*Hebrew, meaning "beginning and end".

You went into a coughing fit, were sedated and then breathed your last, surrounded by all of us.

Thinking back, I only have vague memories of how your lifeless body looked at the wake; your skin was powdery from the make-up and still somehow waxy; your cheeks gaunt from the weight you had lost – everyone remarked how healthy you looked, even though you had been receiving treatment regularly for your illness. And the colour they used on your lips! But of course, nobody commented on this, out of respect. Were you wearing a wig or did they shave off what little hair you had? What colour shirt and tie did you have on? Did I forget because I chose to forget? Or were the details inconsequential that I did not remember?

We used a photo taken at my wedding for your funeral, Dad. You looked dashing and dapper, in a white striped shirt, paired with a light red spotted tie, as you walked me down the aisle of the church and handed me over to R. (I realised, from looking through old photos to pick this one, that I got my awkward smile from you. Unlike Mom, who smiles naturally for posed photographs, somehow, no matter how hard we tried, there would be something about our facial expressions that would be awkward, or sheepish at best.)

Who would have known that 13 months separated the happiest and saddest day of my life?

Actually, if you think about it, weddings and funerals are very similar: Guests sitting at round tables, eating, talking, catching up with friends, relatives, and distant relatives whom one has not seen and probably will never see again after the event. The celebrating/grieving family sits at the front, and guests come up to offer their congratulations or condolences.

Why did I find out you were so proud of me only at your wake? It turned out that you had talked about me all the time to your friends!

They said: "You are the daughter, right? You are the one who writes reviews for the newspapers?"

"Oh yah, you are the music history lecturer! Your father said you could play a lot of instruments."

Even your colleagues said: "You are the one who does triathlon and pole dance! He showed us a photo of you upside down before, saying you were crazy." (When I picked up pole dance in the UK in 2012, before it was accepted in the mainstream, I made sure I was good enough to pose for a photo in an upside-down leg hang before I dared to tell you about my new "sport". Your reaction was anything but what I had predicted!)

But what a time God had chosen to take you away. The week you had left us was also the week all Methodist pastors in Singapore were having their annual retreat. So, no one was available to conduct the wake services except this blundering minister, a self-proclaimed "Reverend", who could not even get your name right.

The day of the funeral was also one of the worst days to go to Mandai Columbarium; it was the weekend of the Qingming Festival, or Tomb-Sweeping Day, and every other family in Singapore was there to pay respects to deceased family members. There was only one way in and one way out of the complex; so, needless to say, a massive bottleneck ensued, resulting in us arriving late for the final rites and cremation.

To make up time, they had left out my eulogy and cut short Matt's, so that we could vacate the space in time. We then watched from above as the coffin was transferred into the fire by a mechanised trolley a few levels down.

***

These days, when I visit the hospital, I am glad I do not have to walk past the chemotherapy suites on the 2nd floor, where we had spent so much time. Instead, I go straight to the 3rd floor where my doctor practises. It is the same order of business each time – first, they take my weight and blood pressure, then they ask me to pee on a stick.

You see, Dad, I am pregnant with your first grandchild: A granddaughter whom you will never meet.

As I sit contemplating my ever-growing belly, 28 weeks pregnant and dealing with all the symptoms expected of a pregnant woman: Heartburn, eczema returning with a vengeance, backaches, insomnia… (Where is that pregnancy glow that everyone speaks of?) – I check things off my to-do list, knowing that it will not be long before baby comes along, changing our lives forever.

In almost seven months, I have done a photoshoot on the pole; played a fund-raiser piano recital; continued to dance, run and cycle; acquired a cot and stroller for baby; tidied up the baby room, and celebrated my 33rd birthday.

Did you have a bucket list too, Dad? Things to do, places to go, or people to speak to before you left? I never knew – I could not tell. You always seemed to do things on a whim: Book a trip for the family; take the family out to dinner at a Korean BBQ place; or buy a new car, just because you felt like it.

Just the other day, while looking through pictures on my phone, I came across my favourite shot of you, taken in 2010.

I remember it was a cold winter's day in Hokkaido; Mum was in the restroom, Matt and I were in a museum gift shop. Suddenly you were nowhere to be found.

When I found you later in the Le Tao shop down the street, you were literally like a boy in a candy shop, eyeing brightly and eagerly the cup of steaming hot chocolate the server behind the counter was preparing for you.

You used to buy gifts for us on a whim too. Work often took you to Vietnam and Thailand, but when you were sent to further places like Korea, you would ask if we wanted anything. Once, in jest, I asked: "Could you buy me an oboe, Daddy?" The weekend after, I received a call from you, saying: "I am standing in this huge music mall in Seoul and I found a shop selling second-hand wind instruments. Is *Lorée* a good brand?" Wow. *Is Lorée a good brand?* That was the most prestigious brand known to my three-month, oboe-playing self at that time!

However, as much as you bought the finer things for us, you also made sure we learnt the value of money, and worked or saved up for the things we wanted. We would be allowed to use some of our Chinese New Year red packet money to fund a goal or buy something nice, but the rest would have to be saved in the bank for the future. In fact, I remember in the few months I spent in junior college, and later while pursuing a diploma, you forbade me from working at Starbucks, even though it seemed the coolest thing to do for extra pocket money. Instead, you suggested that I teach in a music school because of the better hourly pay. Thinking back, that three-year stint had allowed me to hone my teaching skills, giving me a head start after my graduation.

I remember thinking, at that time, "That's not fair!", whenever I saw my classmates further their studies abroad, whereas I could not. As you explained: "You can study as much as you like, as long as you are paying for it."

Working for the next three years – playing piano accompaniment and teaching – gave me the space and time to learn, read, and consider which overseas masters programme I really wanted, instead of taking a masters in Music Performance like everyone else. When I went into your room with acceptance letters from five universities in the UK, plus my bank book as proof I had saved enough, you took out your credit card and said: "Here, book your plane ticket."

The course I eventually chose, Historical Musicology with a minor in Piano Performance, has shaped everything I do today, giving me opportunities to work with different organisations, artists, and students. It lands me in a different place, compared to if I had gone for a masters in Music Performance.

It was only then that I realised how much effort you had put into providing a comfortable, safe environment for us to grow up in. I admired how you had juggled fathering, working and church. To you, there was no such thing as retirement, because there was always something to do. I wished I could have been there more often for you when you were stressed or worried, but you had never shown us that side. You were always strong, always in control. I am grateful for all you had done for the family.

***

In reflecting on my upcoming journey as a parent, I realise parenting skills do not come naturally just because I have a parent, any more than eating many meals will make me a good cook. And so, before even turning to books and self-help material, I started thinking about the way you and Mum had brought us up.

If I had to sum up our relationship, it would be that you had given me 100 per cent freedom to do anything I wanted, yet were willing to step in if you thought I was going in the wrong direction. Hundred per cent freedom and yet, 100 per cent control: How is that possible? I think it is because of the two-way trust that we had had in each other. You trusted me to explore the world, to bloom where I was planted. On the other hand, I trusted that you wanted the best for me, and that there would always be this safety net, knowing that you would protect me from anything you deemed unsafe, especially from things I had yet to understand.

You also taught me to finish what I start, in everything I do, from short-term goals such as Olympic Distance triathlons or 32km races, to years-long mastery of multiple musical instruments to a diploma-level standard. As cheesy as it sounds, it was really not about the end goal but the perseverance and discipline of practice that you had instilled in me.

In dealing with people, you taught me how to under-promise and over-deliver; be kind to others, to have an understated and elegant manner instead of flamboyance; and always give my 100 per cent attention when listening to people because sometimes, they say more in their actions than their words.

Thank you, Daddy, for giving me this environment to grow up in, for being quietly watchful in the background and not interfering. All the time spent with you was never enough, and although I have said this countless times, I love you and you will always be my number one.

Natalie Ng plays the piano, oboe, and violin but preferably not all at the same time. She graduated with a Bachelor of Arts (Hons) in Oboe Performance from the Nanyang Academy of Fine Arts in 2009, and also holds a Masters in Musicology from the University of Leeds. She has given recitals and collaborative performances in various parts of the UK. Upon her return to Singapore, she has written music reviews for *The Straits Times*, and taught music history at Nanyang Academy of Fine Arts.

She is currently a programmer with Esplanade – Theatres on the Bay. Her interests outside of work include multi-disciplinary collaborations in music, literature, art, and photography; she is also an avid pole dancer and triathlete.

My Unfinished Conversation with Papa

Charmaine Leung

Dearest Papa,

This letter is 30 years overdue. There was so much I had wanted to say to you that fateful night 30 years ago. But I did not say a word. I could not. As I saw you lying in a coma in Kwong Wah Hospital's intensive care unit, my mind was blank, devoid of words. My body had felt numbed and till this very day, I still remember the chills down my spine that evening. Was it from remorse that I did not get help fast enough, or was it from the cold February weather in Hong Kong? Then, you left us – exactly 48 hours after your first cry for help, claiming that you could not breathe. I went through your wake and funeral in a daze, not knowing anyone in a rather foreign city; feeling only mildly emotional when your three best friends showed up at the wake. All this had happened in those "cannot-be-forgotten" days of February 1990, which have since become some of the most surreal experiences I have ever had.

It was so long ago, yet it felt like it was just yesterday. Where did all the years go? I have missed you dearly, Papa. Every single day of my life. I have thought about you every day in one way or another. Sometimes, it is your kind smile, or your half-amused, half-annoyed look when you had no clue how to tame the mischievous me. Other times, when I was stuck at some crossroads of an uncharted path, I asked myself how you would have acted and what advice you would have given me. I often wondered if you had not left us so abruptly when I was 17, would you have had such a big impact on my everyday thoughts and life? And, if we did not live in different countries as I was growing up, would you have been in my thoughts as often? Was constantly thinking of you a result of the lack of having you by my side, or because I loved you so? It feels ludicrous that I do not have a definitive answer to these questions. I can only guess that perhaps thinking about you every single day was something I had learnt to do from a young age, simply because you were not there. A learned habit – just like walking and running.

In the blink of an eye, I have grown from the young brooding daughter who used to pen simplistic letters of childish prose, like "how are you", "I am fine", to a free-spirited, independent middle-aged woman who has traversed many journeys – at least, that is what I would like to believe. But I know if you were alive today, I would still be the Daddy's girl who could have you twirled around my little finger, indulging me in my every ask. So much has transpired in the years since you left us. I wish I could have a face-to-face chat to share my tales about the colourful adventures that I have had. I longed for an adult conversation with you, one in which you could get to know the person I have become, speaking as individuals with decades of lived experiences, exchanging ideas and discussing our observations of this thing we call "life".

I distinctly remember the last time we had a "semi-adult" conversation. It was days before you left us. I was deliberating whether to pursue my studies in a university or polytechnic. Prior to that, it had always been you as a grown-up commanding a child, or a doting father pandering to my juvenile requests. That chat was the first time our interaction amounted to anything that resembled a sharing and exchange of thoughts. You had suggested I thought hard about the possibilities of either option, giving me a first lesson on how I should look beyond the obvious when I contemplate life decisions. It was a pity that we could not further that discussion.

Papa, I eventually went to the university. But I did not pursue Accountancy, or follow in your footsteps as an accountant. Instead, I did a degree in Humanities and Social Sciences and learned languages that taught me to appreciate arts and culture. These studies gave me perspectives I never had and taught me to be comfortable in exploring issues and questioning ideas. They altered my world view and taught me to embrace life in a way different from what I had been brought up, providing a new lens for me to experience life and the adventures that it could bring. It was probably in these university years that my curiosity was piqued and I found the will to seek novel experiences in paths less travelled, leading to my eventual decision to explore living overseas.

You must have known how much I adored Hong Kong as a child, so it would be no surprise to you that I took up the offer to work in the city you had called home, when the first opportunity presented itself after my graduation. What you and I probably did not know was how early this seed of wanting to live in Hong Kong had been planted! It was probably during those early years when I had visited you with Mummy. From the yummy roast pigeons at Lung Wah Hotel in Sha Tin, to the bumper car rides at Lai Yuen Amusement Park, or an after-dinner stroll down the bustling Ladies' Market, before returning to our apartment in Sai Yeung Choi Street – every childhood memory I have of Hong Kong was a pleasant one. And for that, I thank you, Papa!

Your sudden and premature departure fuelled my desire to live in Hong Kong. I had felt my ties with you were severed overnight. Literally. Forever. Completely. I hardly knew you as a father, or the man that you were. All I knew were stories Mummy told me in passing – you were the son of a second wife; Grandpa passed away when you were a young boy; Grandma had to leave you in the care of a relative for months on end when she took up work as a housekeeper as she could not bring you along with her. I *had to* find a way to know you – there must be one! I had a strong belief that through knowing more about Hong Kong, I would get to know you – the *real* you that I did not get to meet during those fleeting holidays you took to Singapore to be with Mummy and me during Lunar New Year. I needed to find a way to learn what I could no longer from you directly. I wanted to experience you through living in Hong Kong. This was also my opportunity to "find my roots", having always felt lost in Singapore and wondering if I belonged in another place.

So off I went to Hong Kong in 1997 and made it my home for a good 15 years. I tried to experience Hong Kong in a way that I imagined you had lived it – amongst the locals, speaking their language and adopting their way of life – despite working for an international company and knowing hardly anyone in Hong Kong when I first arrived. I went out of my way to immerse myself in Hong Kong culture and made friends with people from all walks of life. Besides partying and drinking in Lan Kwai Fong like a typical expatriate (which you would probably disapprove of), I also climbed mountains and hiked the trails to soak in Hong Kong's natural landscape which the locals are so proud of. I learnt the way Hongkongers use Cantonese to express themselves and unlearnt Cantonese phrases that would immediately give away my outlander identity.

It was in Hong Kong that I started *really* living. It was in Hong Kong that I grasped much about living, through you – well, the memory of you. Although you were not physically there to show me the way, the memory of you gave me many life lessons. It took me many years – much later – before I realised that prior to Hong Kong, I was merely surviving.

It is ironic how in life, you could not have taught me these things but in death, you taught me so much. Your sudden departure enlightened me to the fact that I must live life to the fullest – as if every day was my last, so that I would have no regrets. Your last words uttered in fear as you were gasping for air – "I do not want to die" – still ring in my ears today. In Hong Kong, I went about life with a vengeance. I lived like there was no tomorrow, taking on new adventures I would otherwise not have ventured into. I must admit it took a bit of trial and error before this became a useful guide. It was only in my later years in Hong Kong that I found an equilibrium to balance free-spiritedness with being sensible, so that I could better experience and appreciate life's highs and lows. Being thousands of miles away from Singapore, I had finally found the beginnings of what I would consider my personal growth journey, which would eventually shape the person that I have become. Papa, I learnt from your home city what you could not be there to teach me, and for that, Hong Kong will always have a special place in my heart.

Since your passing, I would think of you whenever I hear the song "The Living Years" by Mike + The Mechanics. It sounds crazy for me to say I wished we had the opportunity to argue our perspectives. We neither had the experience to not see eye to eye, nor had to talk things through. For many, it would be a blessing to never argue with one's father. For me, it was a void that I could never fill. I did not have you by my side to walk through the passage of life. I often wondered if I would turn out differently had I not lost you so early. I would never know the answer to that. What I know for certain, though, is that I minded very much not having had the opportunity to develop a strong father-daughter bond that would inevitably have come with the lows of disagreements and the highs of reconciliation and understanding. I wished I had the knowledge of the things you held dear and stood for; your hopes and fears that would have helped me comprehend why you and Mummy decided all those years ago to live in different countries. I was constantly told by you and Mummy that the decision was made because it was good for me to be schooled in Singapore. I did not understand it at all. I often wondered if that was the only reason. How could that be the only reason? Even if it were true, I wished you both never told me that was the reason we could not live together. The burden was – and is – heavy. As a child, I had felt guilty that I was the cause of the family's separation; I was the reason for the abnormalities in our family life. Till this day, I sometimes wilfully wished both of you had made a different decision. I blamed Mummy mostly for the decision because she was always there for me to pin the responsibility on. Lucky for you, you were living overseas and then gone too early for me to hold you accountable. But the truth is, Papa, I was angry with you for a long time. It was only in my adulthood that I realised I have been angry with you since I was a child. This happened whenever I was alone with Mummy at school events, while being surrounded by schoolmates who had both their parents with them; when I needed a father figure to look up to and protect me in my teenage years; and when you had abandoned me through your death.

I know the trials and difficulties that I had experienced in my childhood gave me a life path that was unusual. It eventually led me to write a book about growing up in our family. Yes, Papa, I wrote a book and published it – can you believe it? I wished you were there to witness the book launch – I think you would have been proud of me. The most amazing thing about writing a book was it forced me to do a lot of soul searching. It prompted me eventually to have a long overdue "adult" conversation with Mummy. I verbalised my unhealed memories of my difficult childhood and addressed the hurts I had experienced from her. Through this process, I was able to put to rest the demons in my heart and reconciled with her – just like what I am doing with you now, in this letter to you. I am extremely grateful for this opportunity to write to you.

"Talking to you", in this intimate manner, has allowed me to lay down many unresolved thoughts that I had kept locked up for a long time. I have always blamed myself for not helping you fast enough on that fateful night you had a heart attack. I bore the guilt from that night, like how I carried the burden of being the cause of our family's separation.

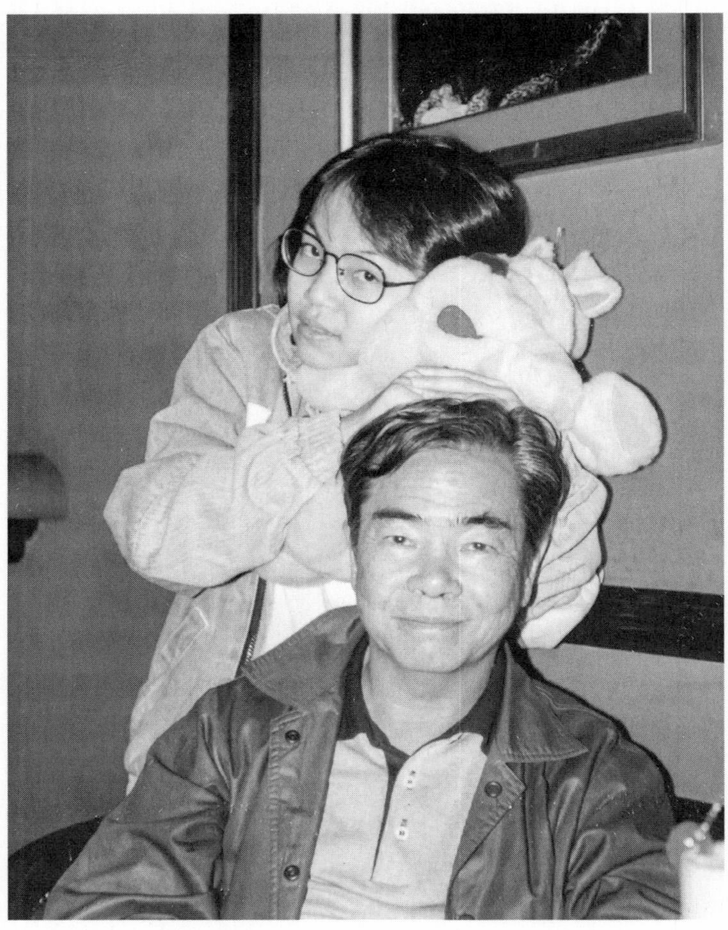

Charmaine and her Papa.

I am sorry, Papa. I wished I had done more for you. But I also realise now I need to free myself and not dwell on what I could never have changed. I should focus instead on what is left that I can do. I know if you were still here today, you would tell me the same too. You have always been the sensible and pragmatic one in the family. What I can promise you now is that I will take good care of Mummy. She is well, but you know what she is like, always nagging and fussing. I will let her have her way – because we know better than to defy her. Just like that, Papa, I feel like I have gone back to those days when you and I used to "conspire" against Mummy, sharing a laugh about how we must give in to her if we want to hear the end of her nagging (laugh!).

All good things must come to an end. This has been a wonderful conversation – albeit a monologue. I am glad I managed to tell you what I could not and did not earlier. Thank you for giving me the gift of life so that I could learn and explore fully life and what it has to offer. I am grateful for all the sacrifices you had made so that Mummy and I could be given the things you thought were good for us. I know it could not have been easy for you at all – being away from your wife and daughter all those years, living alone in Hong Kong, thousands of miles away from us in Singapore. Thank you, Papa, for being the man, husband and father that you were. I love you dearly.

Till we meet again,

Charmaine Leung is the author of *17A Keong Saik Road* – a creative non-fiction book about her childhood in Keong Saik Road when it was a prominent red-light precinct in the 70s and 80s. After a life overseas for almost 20 years, Charmaine returned to Singapore and discovered a vastly different Keong Saik Road. Her childhood and the changes she witnessed upon her return prompted her to pen a memoir of her growing up years. *17A Keong Saik Road* was shortlisted for the Singapore Literature Prize 2018 and has been featured in various panels in the Singapore Writers Festival and talks since its launch in May 2017.

An Education from My Father

Crispin Rodrigues

In the early 90s, before all the nonsense of the devil's triangle and cat murders, Yishun was a town where music reverberated from the block opposite our house, where I could hear the church bells tolling one moment and the *azan* the next. It was in this place that you, Dad, gave me a proper music education.

Music was in our blood. You would tell me when I was a boy: "You need to learn all the classics; some Elvis, some Beatles, and some country music too. No Eurasian ever grew up not listening to Hank Williams." Mom said that because you were a heavy smoker and did not want me to breathe in the smoke, you would never carry me and instead, leave me in the cot next to the radio where you would always have Brian Richmond on Gold 90.5FM playing the oldies. And when I was learning how to speak, you would teach me song lyrics to help me enunciate better.

She loves you, yeah yeah yeah
She loves you, yeah yeah yeah

You became impressed when at age three, I had learnt to sing "Kokomo" by The Beach Boys from watching troll dolls singing it on TV. At six, I knew all the words to "Hotel California" by The Eagles and thought: How scary to be able to check out anytime you like but you could never leave?

You thought it was perfectly fine to not be able to play the recorder, but that I needed to know song lyrics by heart because our culture was embedded in them. When you bought our first family car, a green Fiat Uno, you made sure that you blasted the radio loud during our rides, so that we could sing in the car until I knew the song by heart.

> Picture yourself in a boat on a river
> With tangerine trees and marmalade skies
> Somebody calls you, you answer quite slowly
> A girl with kaleidoscope eyes

So, your taste became my taste and with every passing year, people kept saying that I looked more and more like you. By the time I was in my teens, I had this vast compendium of songs in my head that stretched from Al Jolson to the Backstreet Boys. You would ask me how my day went and I would say, "It is a Good Vibrations day" or "A Rocket Man day". We developed a secret language between us which not even Mom could get into. All our relatives started saying how close we were because we had found this common interest that nobody else knew how to develop between themselves and their children.

Even when my uncles and aunt began moving out of Yishun about the time I was 12, we still remained together because of our common love of music. Uncle Charlie used to run a mobile disco back in the 70s and when he moved to Pasir Ris, he brought along his collection of records. Uncle Philip, you and I would spend time at his place listening to LPs of The Jackson Five and Herb Albert and the Tijuana Brass. Aunt Girlie (whose name was Cecilia but we have always called her Girlie) had also sent us Led Zeppelin CDs, with Robert Plant on the cover looking all suave and sexy with his sweaty bare chest, all the way from her little apartment in York in the UK. Although we might be further apart, it was as if my post-puberty music became a substitute for the stretching veins that circulated in its own network, with you being a placeholder for my own heart, orchestrating what I listened to form the playlist of my youth.

Now I've reached that age
I've tried to do all those things the best I can
No matter how I try
I find my way to the same old jam

Uncle Philip was the first to quit the band, and it was an accident. An incident at PSA port. Large container. Splat. You reached the site first. But no way you could have helped or saved him. After we had buried him at Choa Chu Kang cemetery, you played The Beatles' *The White Album* non-stop until deep grooves cut into the underside of the CD.

While I was serving national service, my taste in music began changing. I had gone to Sembawang Music to purchase albums by Eminem and Dr Dre, Green Day and The White Stripes. On days when I was doing guard duty by myself, I would place a boombox nearby and play "Seven Nation Army" (by The White Stripes) or "Stan" (by Eminem) to keep me awake.

That was the period when I spent the most time away from you and Mom, having to stay in camp half the time. When I made friends with my bunkmates, they would often offer me a side of their earphones so I could listen to what they were listening too. It was like a whole new jukebox had sprung up, unleashing the entire discography of Tupac, like a drive-by, in my mind. Jazz was for old-folks' homes, for people who slow-danced as an exercise in preventing Alzheimer's; musicals were for the elderly to relive their youth. Every month, I made it a point to buy a new artiste whom I had only now heard about. I would play the CD on loop at home – Sonic Youth, The Smashing Pumpkins, Metallica, even slower stuff by the likes of Damien Rice. They represented a coming-of-age in a way that made me distinct from your shadow, Dad. I was finally finding something different and embracing these songs that you are unfamiliar with.

> Today is the greatest
> Day I've ever known
> Can't live for tomorrow
> Tomorrow's much too long

I remember during that time, you used to bang on my door to tell me to keep it down, in case I disturbed the neighbours, before returning to the news on TV. By the time I had emerged from my room for a glass of water, the house would be dark and silent, with a faint leftover smoke from your cigarette, implying that I had only just missed you.

In fact, once we had such a vitriolic argument that you stormed out.

"So, now you think you are better than us, huh?"

"I did not say that."

"Just remember that your Mom and I worked hard to put you through university."

You had left your cigarette on the ashtray so long that it had whittled down to a stub and the ashes were being blown onto the floor.

"It is not that I do not respect you …"

"I do not get you young people these days, thinking that just because you have a uni education you are smarter than us. Can talk down to us like we are idiots."

With that, you left the house, still in your singlet and shorts. You did not come back until I had gone to bed.

I can't stop loving you,
I've made up my mind
To live in memories
Of the lonesome times

Aunty Girlie was the next to go. We received a call one evening after dinner. It was three days before Christmas. Her voice was almost a whisper. Cancer. Breast and bone. The line cut, then Lesley Gore's "You Don't Own Me" started playing on the radio. You and Mom managed to catch her for a couple of days before she left, dead in the middle of winter. I could not go because I had school the next day. You were there for two weeks, settling funeral arrangements. You came back and gave me a poster of *Abbey Road* (The

Beatles' last album). I rolled it up and put it at the back of the cupboard.

During most of my university years, our relationship involved mostly missed connections, with occasional hellos and byes. When I woke for lessons, you had already left for work. When I returned from hanging out with friends after a few drinks, or after a night of social dancing, the lights would be switched off and the only interaction with you would be to shout through the slit in the bathroom door a quick goodnight and wait for your gruff "Goodnight". Other than that, we hardly talked much and by my final year as an undergraduate, I did not realise that you had already sprouted your first grey hairs until Mom told me in passing one day.

Uncle Charlie was the last to go. It was sudden. The ICU. The heavy breathing. Fading in and out. His eyes flickered at me, and his thin lips broke into a smile. I whispered in his ear that I would try to keep the music going. Everyone was crying, you holding his hand, not wanting to let go. But we had to, eventually. He was buried as per Muslim rites, and with his Muslim name.

In the car, you and I looked at our mud-soaked shoes and for the first time ever in my life, I saw you cry. It was a very repressed attempt at keeping quiet, like a cat mewling in pain. You tried to shield your face from me, but I could see your mouth contorted, as if you had broken your jaw trying to stifle a bawl. It was the sudden realisation that the band had broken up and you were its sole member. On our way home, we switched off the radio and said nothing.

When we reached home, I went into my room and worked on my final-year paper on Bob Dylan. In the background, I played "Knockin' on Heaven's Door" softly on my laptop. It was work, or perhaps my feeble attempts at closure. That night, after I returned home from supper with friends, I found Uncle Charlie's record player and a small pile of Dylan records on my bed. That night, I cried.

Mama put my guns in the ground
I can't shoot them anymore
That cold black cloud is comin' down
Feels like I'm knockin' on heaven's door

The next day, I left my door open so that you, still sleepy-eyed, would chance upon me setting up the record player, drawing an extension cord across the room until it was situated next to the window, surrounded by a few potted plants.

"You know, your Uncle Charlie really liked Bob Dylan."

I nodded.

"I never could see why though."

I nodded.

"But maybe if you tell me why, I would be willing to agree to disagree."

And so, we sat together for the next few hours, listening while arguing about the value of Dylan's polemics against interpretation, and agreed to disagree. I told you about the paper I was working on and how much of his argument I was going to plagiarise and offer as my own. It was the first conversation in two years we had had that lasted more than 10 minutes. I eventually finished the paper three months after Uncle Charlie's passing. At my graduation ceremony, I finally apologised to you. You had said that I had done it for all of us,

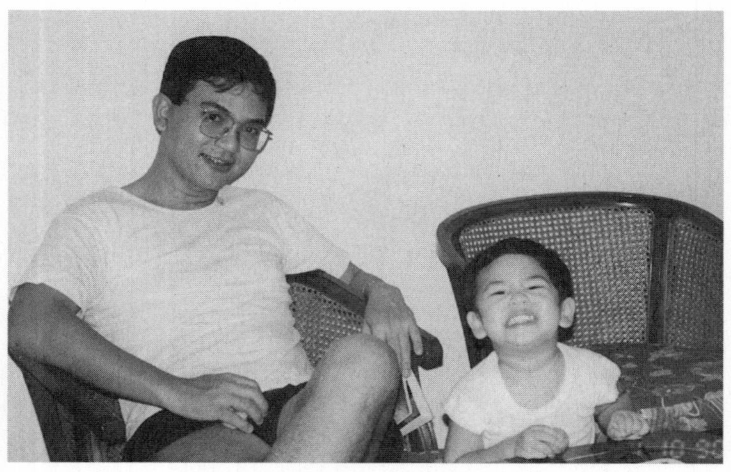

A young Crispin (right) and Dad pose for a photo.

for you and your siblings. My professor, who had dropped by, said how much I was the spitting image of you.

This past Christmas, you bought me a new record player and a first edition of *The White Album.* They sit nicely next to Uncle Charlie's record player, surrounded by potted plants.

Blackbird singing in the dead of night
Take these broken wings and learn to fly
All your life
You were only waiting for this moment to arrive

To live with you, Dad, is to receive an education in music. When you laugh, the room thunders with the bassline and authority of your three siblings, all gone but never forgotten. When you sing, I imagine the four of you, cigarettes in hand, sitting by the record player, cradling me and cooing me to sleep. I have now grown accustomed to smoke and it smells like love.

Dad, you have given me an education and, in return, I have learnt that despite your inability to speak of love, you have learnt to love Bob Dylan, or Eminem, or Taylor Swift instead, and that, in itself, is sufficient to drown out cat deaths and a devil's triangle. In your neighbourhood, with its cacophony and playlist long enough to last a lifetime, none of us have ever left Yishun.

Crispin Rodrigues is the author of *Pantomime* and *The Nomad Principle*, both published by Math Paper Press. He is also the co-editor of the anthology *Crazy Little Pyromaniacs*, an anthology of young Singapore poets 35 years old and below.

Flamenco and Leopard Print: Memories of Childhood

Jacintha Abisheganaden

Dad, I remember you bought a little cottage, now called a bungalow, at 108 Thomson Rise when I was growing up. It came with every imaginable fruit tree growing in the garden, like rambutan and starfruit. There was a huge *belimbing* tree outside my room and even a lime bush in the back garden.

At the gate, we had jasmine, which would bloom at night and we would find scattered petals all over the driveway by the morning. It was my job to collect a few limes for curries and the *kebun*'s (gardener) job to fill a sack-full of *belimbing* for himself, as he could climb that tree.

At some point, you had installed a goal post at the end of the short garden, so my brother and his friends could play football.

Mother never minded. She would cook a roast chicken once a week for Sunday lunch. It was part of her strict "English" diet of frozen minute steaks, mashed potatoes and Campbell's soup for us as she wanted us to grow "tall".

Mother had gone to school at Fairfield Methodist, but her education was disrupted by the war. Later, she managed to get a scholarship to study in London and then lectured at the teachers' training college.

Despite her studies abroad, she liked to wear matching sets of Thai silk cheongsams with little box jackets that had buttons the size of dollar coins. If you opened her cupboard, you would find, stuck to the inside of the door, her next week's schedule of cheongsams from Monday through Friday. You would read descriptions such as "green Thai silk, plum lace, blue Thai silk". If the cheongsams were plain, the coats would sometimes be printed with flowers or odd Cubist designs that were "in" in the 60s.

On weekends, Mother took to her sewing machine to do drapes, dresses and runners for the table. But she was not in the least domesticated. Sometimes, halfway through cooking, her hyperthyroidism (a condition in which the body produces too much of the hormone thyroxine, resulting in weight loss or irregular heartbeat) would kick in (she has been 46kg all her life) and she would be exhausted and disinterested. The maid would then have to take over from her desultorily.

Mother never ate desserts and was usually asleep by 9pm. And she was rather vocal, even for a woman in the 60s, about contraceptives for men in China as they began their one-child policy.

When Mother got mad, she would yell at you in Cantonese and if she was driving, she would be driving really fast. Her brother, my Uncle Richard, had once competed in the first Grand Prix in Singapore, with Grandfather building the car from scratch. Mother always drove more stylishly than you, who drove like a musician, thinking more of a tune rather than the road.

There were usually three cars in the driveway and it seemed always a clutch of cellists in the living room, practising for one of my Uncle Paul's cantatas.

We often came home from school to live classical music. No wonder I started singing on television with friends, though for my brother, he decided to take up riding horses.

When I was nine, I remember Elisabeth Gaye Hebdige swanning into our driveway in her Jaguar Mark 10 with you, Dad, as her driver. She spoke with a Spanish accent and was married to an Englishman who was in banking. They lived in a huge bungalow in Garlick Avenue.

Once, Pete and I tagged along to a rehearsal at her home and found, once the front door was opened, a marbled foyer with flowers in a giant vase, like what you would see in a hotel, leading to a winding staircase down to the living room, and then a large swimming pool.

I was in heaven. And when she opened the screen doors to what might be the first Japanese-inspired room, with tatami mats, rice screens and heavy wood, I thought it was the chicest thing to have a Japanese room.

It was there that you conducted the rehearsal that day, while we played by the pool.

From what I remember, Elisabeth liked to wear mostly catsuits of leopard print. That was because she was Spanish, Mother had said by way of an explanation.

You had been practising the Catellan songs, Dad, whenever she dropped by our place. "Ah-Lexxe," she would purr, entering our humble abode in what I can now see as a flurry of extravagance-meeting-serendipity. I then vowed to make entrances with castanets and stilettos from that day.

I would be fiddling with my portable turntable in my room, in full view of a very beautiful Spanish woman with very red lipstick singing Spanish songs. If I ventured out, she would smile at me and continue singing.

I surmised, at that young age, that a classy woman is one who must be friendly to children.

Elisabeth's voice had a burnt, brittle quality to it, like seared scallops. Out of the air, she would pull castanets curled in each palm like shells, viciously beating a subplot to her singing. Alongside the castanets and her smoky, steely voice, she would drum out a dance rhythm in golden strapped high heels.

Dad, you played nice flamenco, especially with a guitarist's hands – the left one with nails trimmed, the right hand with long nails for flamenco. Thrum tatarum tatarum tatarum tata Rum Tata rum tatarum Tata rum ta ta RUM... and then into the intro of the song, which was always a bit of a lament before it got hot and thrumming again.

Sometimes, you would beat on the wooden body of the guitar, with the chords in place. Rather stormy, macho stuff. "Ah-Lexxe," Elisabeth would say, "let's take it again from the second verse."

Upon reflection, Dad, you playing flamenco, with this creature in a leopard catsuit singing, has become the musical score forever burnished in the hallways of my childhood, a magical mystery tour of high glamour from a mansion in Bukit Timah to the hills of Seville.

Together with chamber groups, with whom you played double bass, you had performed in many concerts at the Victoria Theatre and the RELC (Regional English Language

Centre), for soirées in moneyed homes and on radio and TV.

Elisabeth would often speak of the hills and countryside of Granada just before singing. She would wear gowns with billowing chiffon sleeves and trains. After your day job as a Group Inspector of Schools, you would turn up in a white tuxedo with bow tie, a rosy-brown handmade Jose Ramirez guitar in hand, and your sheets of music.

In the cold auditorium, I would be watching you but feeling sleepy, with school the next day. But I have always known you have a buffet of world-class talent which began with your guitar case in the backseat of your car.

You accompanied her at all her recitals and she was the most thrilling thing to watch, with that Latin fierceness, cheekbones and all. It was a musical collaboration that lasted till she left the country. I thought it was the most glorious time of your life, Dad.

After I became a jazz singer, Elisabeth invited me in 2005 to sing at Asia House in London, where she now lives. I would put on an adequate show, with Jamie Cullum's bassist in my band and all. But it was nothing like the swag, wit and wonder of what Lady Elisabeth had brought to the small living room of my childhood.

I read once that actress Uma Thurman had spoken of her hippie parents always having poets and actors around in the house. Though you and Mother were not hippies, you did give us this bohemian rhapsody of fantastical creatures who came to sing Spanish songs and play Chopin and Sibelius after school. Everyone was always laughing; Kelvin Lim on violin, Brendan Richards on viola, Douglas something or other on

Jacintha is accompanied by her dad on the guitar.

cello. And then, roaring into the driveway, after teaching at the university, in his open-top yellow Rolls Royce, would be large and shy David Rawlinson.

He would give us rides down the road, with us standing on the little runner board which they had for that model, while I held the door, with my brother on the other side.

Once David Rawlinson, who only ever wore brown shoes, played double bass in his black socks because the shoe call that evening was black. In a strange twist of fate, I had brought bassist Joshua Wan to play for me at the New Zealand Arts Festival. He had gotten a bout of gout (from too many blue cheese sandwiches, which he seemed to enjoy in Wellington). So, that night, he could not fit into his shoes. He ended up playing for me in his black socks and I remember the David Rawlinson story from your time.

You had such cool friends from the Young Musicians' Society, though you were older than most of them. After the show, stories would emerge of the famous after-show suppers that would end at three in the morning. Sometimes, you would go to Fatty Weng at Albert Street where you could also order beer.

It was a fine time to be growing up amongst your friends, Dad, these fantastical, friendly creatures who were kind to me, goddesses and fellows of the orchestra. It was a fine thing to watch you have so much fun, Dad.

Jacintha Abisheganaden is a founding member of TheatreWorks Singapore. She is currently a jazz audiophile recording artist with GrooveNote Records USA, with nine titles available on platforms such as Amazon and Spotify. She performs live for shows for both Singapore and internationally. No stranger to television, Jacintha was a full-time actress and host with Mediacorp Channel 5 for four years and a former journalist with *The Straits Times*.

My Father, My Heart*

Kelvin Tan

> The righteous man walks in his integrity;
> His children are blessed after him.
>
> *Proverbs 20.7*

Dear Dad,

This has been a strange and poignant year. But life goes on at home, as usual.

Two days ago, on Sunday, as always, I cleaned the house in the morning, after Mum had gone for a shower. (I vacuum and mop the floor, like you used to. Except that I do not go down on all fours to mop.)

After that, I set the YouTube online church service for her, before going out to buy lunch for us. And dinner after. I do not ask Mum what she wants to eat, like you used to. I just get what I think she likes.

---

* Dedicated to my mother, Madam Lo Phaik In, and also Kenny, Selina, Karen, Swee Chong, Rachel, Olivia, and my dear Jacq.

Now that you are gone, it is just Mum and me at home. I try to look out for her, like how you had always taken such good care of her. The heart-warming way you loved Mum taught me how I should love Jacq.

Mum is doing well, in spite of the virus, and all that has happened here, and in the world. So many people have died, Dad. Many more will. When I think of those who died, I think of you.

What is death, Dad? Do we really die? Is there really such a thing as death? I haven't a clue.

Somehow, for me, you are not really dead, Dad, even though it has been three years since you have been gone.

I know Mum misses you. She tells me sometimes she cries before she sleeps.

I know I miss you too. While I was vacuuming the carpet, below the chair you used to sit on, memories of you came back to me.

Memories that are not necessarily pleasant.

We found it difficult to see you, someone whom we loved and still love, sliding into such a debilitating illness in your last few years, as we witnessed your mind and body waste away in a matter of months.

Every day and night, I would observe you on that chair, writhing and groaning in agony, losing your memory bit by bit, staring blankly at the ceiling. We tried to make you feel as comfortable as possible. But to no avail. That sense of helplessness will haunt me for the rest of my life.

We knew it would be a matter of time before you would be forever gone from us. Forever lost.

I remember the day I found out you had left us, Dad. I

was doing my routine long walk near home, and making my way back from Ghim Moh, when Kenny called and paused for quite a while, before exclaiming: “Dad’s gone.”

I rushed to the hospital and there you were, lying lifelessly, one of your eyes slightly open.

As Karen was stroking your forehead, I broke down and wept uncontrollably for the longest time I have ever wept in my life. Jolted by the intense sobbing, I just kept staring into your eyes, wondering if you were really dead.

A part of me was relieved you had finally passed. It was hard to see you suffer so much.

I remember not crying anymore after that. I still do not know why, Dad.

As they pushed your coffin into the incinerator, the intense outpouring of emotion filled the cold and hollow space of the crematorium. I had never seen Rachel weep so much.

But I did not cry at all. Maybe I had gotten that trait from you? It is amazing how fast you would get over any kind of disappointment or grief.

How did you do it, Dad? Was it because you had to leave school so young to support Mama, that you learned to deal with whatever life threw at you?

I once asked you if you had regretted dropping out of school so early but you just shrugged it off, saying that you just had to do what you had to do. You just got on with life, Dad. And you always did the very best you could in all that you did.

As the years pass, I tend to reflect on our life, our relationship. The more I think about who you were and are, the more I realise that so many of your traits remain in me.

It is even in this letter to you.

The clear and concise English that you were such a master of, and the way you expressed yourself so succinctly, are evident in my writing here. But as I have learnt through time, no one can write clearly or concisely, until one knows exactly what one wants to say. For that to happen, one has to be honest.

Honest. That was what you were, Dad. You were all about The Truth.

Remember when I was about 10, we were shopping in a supermarket at Beach Road? I was caught by the guard for shoplifting, and you had to follow me into the office to be questioned by the management.

I was terrified because I had honestly forgotten to pass the item that I had wanted to buy to you to be paid. After I convinced the guards that I had made a mistake, I was let off.

When we had dinner later, you spent a long time asking if I had told the truth: "You might have lied to the manager, but you can tell me the truth. If you really did shoplift, tell me. I will not be angry and punish you. All I want is the truth."

It was the single greatest lesson you, or anyone, could have ever taught me. Because of you, I have spent, and am spending, my life searching for the truth. Perhaps that is why I have always had a soft spot for writers like Hemingway and Carver. In clear, simple sentences, they wrote, profoundly and truthfully.

Thank you for showing me how to live a life of integrity. You wore your integrity like a badge of valour. And you did not mind what I did in life, as long as I am a good and honest person.

All that I am, as a creative person, as an artist, is because of you. Art is my means of searching for my own truth. A search that you had put in me. I would not have been a writer if you had never encouraged me to read and write well.

You were around my age now, when I started my life at the National University of Singapore. I remember you were so glad I had made it. You used to tell me because you and Mum did not have wealth, all you could have given us was an education. And it was the greatest gift you could have ever given us.

But you also gave me so much more. They say that a good and exemplary father has the ability to encourage and steer a child to develop the courage and ability to realise his or her vision of his or her own life and to pursue it. Dad, by believing in me, you had, in turn, made me believe in myself.

You always made me feel secure, even when I was going through dark periods in my life.

And I have never lost sight of what my vision of life is, and should be, no matter how much of a struggle it has been. And it has been a meaningful struggle, thanks to you, Dad.

You had never disapproved of my career choice, even when you knew that I was going to take the hard road of pursuing an artistic life, one that would be uncompromising, uncertain and idealistic.

In fact, you helped me edit my first novel and even pay for the printing. When I started playing music, writing songs, playing in The Oddfellows, releasing my albums in a country that barely had a music industry – or even a thriving arts scene back then – you always gave your support and approval.

You genuinely just wanted me to do what made me happy. As long as I was honest.

That word again. Do you know how rare this trait is in the

world today, Dad? The world could do with more people like you. People who live honestly, and who love the truth.

Other traits you had: You never broke promises. You were always punctual, reliable, and gave of your best in all that you did. You were also generous. "What would I not do for my family" was your favourite quip. Indeed, you always gave all you had for the family. So much so that you worked for over 30 years in the same job, so that we could be well provided for. Thank you, Dad.

You were always resolute, firm and self-assured. Always dealing with challenges calmly, encouraging others to just keep on. It was what you did very well and it showed in your passion, whether it was walking, botany, or anything to do with language, be it writing, journalism, copywriting and editing. That passion to do what one loves, has rubbed off on me.

Most of all, Dad, and I am not sure you had even known about it, you were an idealist. And that idealism has influenced, shaped and transformed my life. For the better, I believe.

But you could also be very tough, Dad. While you were always kind and gracious to people, once they crossed the line, you would become that intimidating, angry man. All of us never wanted to be on the wrong side of your anger when you lost your temper.

Now, I see the sense of that. Give a person 10 chances, but if they mess up the 11th time, retaliate. Do not ever be a pushover. Pure gold, Dad.

I miss the times when we would sit around the huge rosewood table at the old place and just talk about anything under the sun, and laugh a lot. Still, there were also tensions between us, as there will be between all fathers and sons.

I yelled at you once and you never talked to me for weeks, until I wrote you a letter of apology. After that, it was as if we had never fought.

With you, Dad, there was no manipulation, no politics. No nonsense. You were who you were, and you did not muck around.

They say that when someone misses a loved one who has passed, the deceased would appear in dreams. But I have never seen you in my dreams, Dad. Nor have I seen your ghost.

Do I miss you? No. Because you are everywhere. As far as I am concerned, you never left. I once told my friends Krishnan and Deborah, that as long as I live, talk and write about you, like I am now, you will never die.

You will forever live in those who have been blessed by you. You live, because I live.

A few years ago, I went into the studio and recorded three purely improvised albums and dedicated them to you. Here is a song, "My Father", from one of the albums:

I'm lost again
and I don't know where it will all go.

I'm lost again
it seems that no one can help me.

I'm losing touch
with anything that seems to hurt me.

and I don't know where to go

it seems that I am lost in a dialectic,
that brings me nowhere.

and the dusk goes into the darkness
and I'm looking for some comfort that isn't there.

and i feel myself falling through the cracks.
and i feel my soul smashing into smithereens

and daddy you're not there.

and I can't understand the meaning of it all
I can't understand anything
No one reaching out to me at all

and I don't understand the struggle
and I don't understand what it means
and I don't understand where it's going

and all I hope is for mercy
that would save me from purgatory

of living too much in the darkness
of living too much in pain
and living too much in meaninglessness.

all I ask is for mercy
to free me from this darkness

free me from this pain
all ask is for some relief
and where will it come?
it comes from remembering you
my father
it comes from connecting to your soul.
my father
it comes from remembering
remembering your goodness
it comes from remembering you
it comes from spiritually embracing you
it comes from being grateful for you
it comes from loving you
it comes from trying to be like you
it comes from believing in good
it comes from doing good
it comes from celebrating you
it comes crying over you
it comes from trying to say that I miss you
it comes from loving you
it comes remembering you
God bless
Till we meet again.

I remember after recording those albums, how I had felt a burden lifted away from me. It was beautiful.

May God always nestle you in His loving arms.

Love you forever, Dad. Amen.

Kelvin Tan is a musician and writer. Besides being the lead guitarist for seminal homegrown band The Oddfellows, he has released over 150 albums that are available on Spotify and Bandcamp. He is the author of *All Broken Up And Dancing* (1992) and *The Nether(r);R* (2001). His play, *Flights Through Darkness*, was adapted into a film by Wong Kwang Han, and was screened at the 2017 Jogjakarta Film Festival and the 2017 Asian International Film Festival. In 2018, he composed and performed the theme song, "Jie", for the Singapore Writers Festival. Kelvin can be reached at metiokos@hotmail.com.

Kelvin Tan visits his dad's niche at the columbarium.

My Father – A Piece of Heaven

Usha Pillai

When did my sister and I start calling you Father? Here we are, a Malayalee family, where fathers are usually called *Accha*, or *Acchan*, Pa or the more modern Daddy. How in the world did we end up calling you Father, like you had stepped out of a church in liturgical gear, and we were bowing to you?

Father – there is something very stoic about this appellation, but it suited you. For you were not one to show your emotions easily to all of us. Perhaps it had started as a third-person reference, like "he is our father". When I was young, the sound had rolled off my tongue easily, but while I was growing up, it suddenly felt awkward. But Father it remained, till the end of your days.

Father, you used to drive me crazy with your impeccable routine. How could you – or any human, for that matter – be so disciplined? I felt I could never match up to you. For example, all your meals, from breakfast, lunch, tea to dinner, were all taken at the same time, every day. And for every meal, the same amount of rice and curries, ending off with yoghurt

– you knew the exact amount you could stomach. There was no trace of greed or craving for anything more. Even if *Amma* had cooked something yummy, you did not ask for snacks – nothing. You just knew when to stop.

Of course, your diabetic condition had made you very conscious about your sugar intake and you followed the doctor's regimen strictly, like a schoolkid under detention. And every morning after breakfast, you had your "journalist moments" with *The Straits Times*, talking about news bits to yourself, followed by the rendezvous with your table, where you sat to pay bills, note down the calls you needed to make and other to-dos.

(Father, when I was trying frantically to settle your bills after your passing, I confess that there was one pink letter – a late payment notification – in the mail. Forgive me for this blemish on your perfect-citizen record.)

Do you know what the icing on the cake was? You continued this routine even after you had mild dementia. You could forget where you were, where your family was, which country you were in, but you never failed to follow your 8am, 1pm, 4.30pm and 8pm routine for meals! I admired you for this, but it was not something I could keep up.

You used to chide us for this sometimes and got a little rattled when we could not keep our things in order, as you expected the best from us. It was unnerving and, at times, I used to hide from you but it had taken time for me to understand you. That under this strict disciplinarian, there was also a man who was soft, with so much love in him.

Father, although you were not very open with your feelings, you could love, and you showed it in subtle, unexpected ways.

I remember one evening I was unwell. You saw me resting on the sofa in the hall and lit the lamp for evening prayers. You would normally ring the bell, as was the daily practice in temples during the *arathi* (offering of fire from wicks soaked in oil). But that day, you entered the shrine, prayed, and exited quietly. You said: "I didn't ring the bell today. God will understand." What could be more sincere and unconditional than a parent's love?

Another time, I had donated blood and received a small towel with the words "we love blood donors". When I showed it to you, you said, with a big grin: "I also love blood donors." I almost did a double take, as I was unused to you expressing yourself like that! These shows of love slowly took shape in other ways. When your weakness and dementia kicked in, numerous were the times when you needed me to do something for you or explain something to you. Or you just wanted to share a revelation with me. Then I would hear "Usha", "Usha", throughout the day. While this sometimes bothered me, even as I was deep in my important trying-to-juggle-my-fast-paced-life, I slowly realised this, too, was love. You were calling the name of the person whom you knew would respond and be there. Sometimes, you forgot who I was, but you knew my name. And you trusted me to be there.

Once, you had written me a note which I will never forget. During this period, both you and *Amma* never remembered you were actually at home and every evening, would ask to "go home". And you thought you needed money, if not you would be asked to leave. One day, I clarified that you did not need to leave and that I had money. Then you wrote this note to me: "Usha, you really sprang a wonderful surprise. I was almost thinking we made a mistake – and (would be asked to) get out! But God is great. Long live Usha." Within brackets, you added: "(Too Tired) – Father".

My heart melted, for so many reasons. Firstly, your language was still lucid! How was that possible, Father? At 96, you had dementia. Secondly, you probably feared being asked to "get out" every evening – even though no one was chasing you out – and this saddened me. Thirdly, I could sense your love for God, and fourthly, your love for me.

Father, are you happy now? They say good people go to heaven when they die. I have always pictured that you would be there one day, that heaven is a physical place, whitish with clouds and beautiful angels, like what we see in the movies. But now I know that you yourself were a piece of heaven in our lives. Heaven is not a place where good people go when they die. Heaven is what beautiful people bring into our lives when they are here with us on our earthly sojourn. When someone makes us happy, safe, secure, and at peace, how can that not be heaven? For throughout my growing up years, I never felt that I would not be taken care of, or that you would leave me to fend on my own, or that you would stop loving me, even in your 90s when you were diagnosed with dementia. You had brought heaven to us, with your child-like interactions and innocence. You did not have to go to heaven; you ensured that home was heaven for us.

Father, *Amma* began developing dementia almost 10 years ago, the first time it had hit our family. I knew you had trouble understanding it, and found the news hard to accept. I was barely coping with it, and only slowly managed to make sense of it. Then the inevitable happened in December 2018.

For one thing, you were becoming weaker, and my sister and I were getting worried. But a random conversation with you sparked off a greater worry.

You had said something about China's leadership changing hands. And you were sure – even adamant – about it. Even as an avid reader who sometimes could not keep up with the news, I knew it was wrong and that something was wrong. And that something was going to change everything for the next one and a half years.

The doctor had diagnosed mild dementia. But somehow, compared to *Amma*, it was different for you. For one thing, you were still independent and mobile. And, as always, your routine was unbroken, right down to how you sat so still and chanted your daily prayers. No one would have believed your diagnosis when they heard you pray. But the slips in your conversations betrayed you. You began speaking of an exciting life – travelling; attending conferences; waking up in hotels in Sri Lanka or Indonesia; re-living your journalist's life – in another dimension in your mind. Every morning when you woke up, you said you had returned from a different country. I used to balk, argue with you, then try to "knock sense" into you. But dementia has a way of punching you in the stomach, as if to say: "Hey, now you're in my world."

I finally realised that I could not bring you back to the "normal" world. This was your new world now and I had to invite myself in. In this world, I made pretend calls to your friends who had passed on, as you were upset they did not contact you; in this world, I found you standing outside my door at midnight, asking what happened to the "seminar" and where were the "speakers"; in this world, you agonised over so many things, and found relief only in knowing that you were safe in this house; in this world, you and *Amma* held hands more often than I had seen my whole life. In this world so much of your inner nature and personality emerged. An honest man with love, and discipline, and you expected the same from others. Dementia did not diminish you, it made you real.

I truly felt that you and *Amma* lived blissfully together in these last few years, each not realising you had - and that your partner had – dementia. For what you do not know cannot hurt you, right? Each living in their own world and sometimes, in each other's world. I also think that you and *Amma* must have conspired at some point, in some dementia-space you had created together, to drive me a little crazy once in a while. Just like how my sister and I used to drive you both a little – okay, a lot – crazy when we were young, and ignorant.

In fact, I swear sometimes both of you deliberately talked to me *together, at the same time,* about something that happened today, what food to cook, an old friend who passed away. My head would swivel left to right, right to left, like at a tennis match, not knowing whom to pay attention to! Father, I can almost picture you saying: "All those years, you and your sister did this to us. Ah, sweet revenge exacted. Too bad we cannot do this to your sister because she always comes with her husband or kids. Never mind, you will do."

Throughout the illness, your physical strength was declining. Whenever you fell down, nothing in your body broke, but a little part of my heart did. I know that only God could have been there to catch you before you hit the floor – how else could I have explained you getting only slight bruises? He favoured you, as you were so devoted to Him. However, He also missed you and was planning for your extended visit. You were also waiting; you would joke that your passport was ready, you only needed the visa to be chopped (stamped)!

July 12, 2019 – your visa was being prepared. That fateful night, you were sitting on the bed after the helpers had propped you up from the floor. My heart broke. I saw you with some broken teeth, blood on the floor and your t-shirt. But you were talking away with your usual innocence, maybe nonchalance, as if nothing happened, and I had to comfort the emotional helpers: "He is okay *lah*. He is still talking. If he is not talking, then worry."

Your hospital stay after that was agonising, I know – short of slapping the nurses, you made it clear that you did not appreciate their constant questions and tests. Like a beast trapped, you were yanking out your tubes at night to "escape". And you missed *Amma*. When she came in for her last moments with you, both of you held hands, like star-crossed lovers knowing you would not meet again. But, we did not know this then. One doctor expressed surprise that you did not feel the pain from a fractured hip and a silent heart attack which happened in hospital. I told him that you were well taken care of by powers beyond the medical. I also knew your departure was meant to be as painless as the life you had given us while you were alive.

On July 19, 2019, your visa was finally chopped, and you were ready to leave. The nurse had summoned us to the hospital in the wee hours of the morning: "His blood pressure is dropping." You were supposed to return home the day before, but to a bedridden life – one which I dreaded, as I knew you would not be able to handle it. So, there you lay on the bed, lost in another world, eyes peacefully shut, trying hard not to have to open them again. Your BP was slowly dropping. Very, very slowly. It was almost seven hours since we received the call. They say the soul finds it hard to leave when loved ones are around, due to the strong attachment. So, just after 9am you waited till I got distracted by some movement in the ward and I turned back to look – how quickly you grabbed this chance and made your final escape! When I turned back to look at you – it seemed you were pretending to sleep, but I knew that you had gone. The final piece of my heart broke.

Father, sometimes, I am glad you are not here today because you would be utterly anxious about Covid-19. You would be following the daily rise in number of cases and wondering whether your family members in India were safe. And whether your long-gone friends were in good health. You would have asked me to call them, and I would have to make my pretend calls. Every day, you would be cursing some politician or complaining about irresponsible Singaporeans who broke the rules. You would worry about me going to work – would I get infected? Would some colleague pass it to me? All this would have worn out your weary mind and body.

But I also feel sad you did not get to see the changing face of Singapore politics – how much more colourful and vibrant it is. And how Mr Trump, whom you found an awkwardly amusing politician, is no longer in power. Your heart would have skipped with joy and you would have

Usha shares a meal with Dad.

made some snide comment – hah! The journalist in you never died, even with your failing memory. You sat there every morning, *The Straits Times* in your hands. Every. Single. Day. I wanted to use you as my role model for all the young people in my life. When your eyes were failing, I had stopped the ST subscription. But you looked lost without it. When we went for your medical appointments, you would pick up the papers and glance through, even though I knew you could not read the fine print. That was when I decided to re-subscribe the newspapers, because holding the paper in your hands every morning for almost an hour was a routine I should never have disturbed.

Father, is there anyone at all who feels they have not done enough for someone, when that someone passes on? Should

I feel the same, father? Well, perhaps I could have curbed my "inner grumbling" when you called "Usha" to share a 15-minute story that never happened. But that would have made me unreal. This is who I am and this is how you were.

You were my father: Sweet, disciplined, real, and I love you.

Usha Pillai, an educator, has been staying with her parents, together with a string of helpers, since her mum had a hysterectomy. She and her sister Uma have been taking care of them for years. After their father's passing in 2019, a female powerhouse continues to reside in the house – the author, her mother, the current helper and their cat.

Was I Wrong to Let You Go?

Andrew Koh

Your grandson showed me two medals not long ago. I had won them when I was training as a police officer all those years ago. One was a gold medal for a basketball inter-squad competition; the other for being the best officer in interpersonal skills. That was in 1984 and I was completing my training at the Police Academy. You never came to my graduation then.

Pa, it is strange. I had never thought to follow in your footsteps. All the movies about fathers wanting their sons to take over their business, and sons aspiring to emulate their dads, I had watched, but could never relate to them. They were only make-believe. Yet, there I was, a police officer, just like you were all those years ago. That is about the extent I knew of your life before I existed, Pa. A bloody sad admission, if anyone were to ask me.

1988: I was still studying for my degree and a friend drew my attention to a song by Mike + the Mechanics, "The Living Years", written by BA Robertson. The opening bars were distinctive enough for me to remember them still, including the opening line: "Every generation blames the one before." However, the words that best describe how I feel now about you, about us as father and son, are these:

Oh, crumpled bits of paper
Filled with imperfect thought
Stilted conversations
I'm afraid that's all we've got

But who am I being dishonest with, Pa? There were no bits of paper, crumbled or otherwise, no capture of the fleeting thoughts. Our conversations were not long enough to be stilted. Could our talks be even described as "conversations", Pa? And that is all I have now of you, fragments of an already fragmented narrative and a rapidly fading memory. Time and tide do not just flow by; they erode the sands of self.

I do recall asking you about your father. You had said he was rich, owned properties in Shanghai but lost them all when he fled the country in the turmoil. You were born in Singapore and grew up here. You joined the police force as a young man, when the country was still a colony. (What drew you to it? How did you feel about your son becoming a police officer?)

That was how you had met Ma. Her family lived in Lorong Tai Seng, quite a kampong back then. Even I remember that as a child, when Ma used to take me there to visit Ah Ma. The wooden boards with peeling paint – light blue. Concrete floor. Zinc roof that resounded in the heavy rain. The entire house sat on concrete floor. Next door was a huge compound and a house belonging to a Malay family. Chickens ran about on the sandy ground and I had played there with my cousins and the Malay boys. Just in front of Ah Ma's house, was a little pavement. I used to train my reflexes with the *sapu lili* (a bunch of thin rattan bundled up as a broom), hitting as many flies as I could. Surely, when you first patrolled the area and eyed Ma, the kampong must have been more underdeveloped than that. How did you get on with your father-in-law? I heard you respected Ah Ma but I had never seen you visit her. Never saw you back in that environment where you had fallen in love. Things had strained by then, didn't they?

I heard stories from Ma about how you once had ghostly encounters during your time in the police. Your colleague saw *her* as a pillion rider on your bicycle. For days thereafter, you were ill, and it was a horrible time to be ill. Medical facilities were unlike today, of course, but, like today, also expensive, given the poverty level most families were at. Travelling to a clinic would have been difficult too. (Wasn't that how Ah Ma had lost her second daughter as an infant? She did not get to bury her child.) Obviously, you had recovered. It seemed that was not the only time you had experienced or seen spirits. You had intimated as much to me but I had not asked more when I should have.

***

Some of the stories you had told me were fascinating. For instance, secret societies back then had unwritten rules among themselves. They were organised criminal gangs who would lay down their lives for their bosses because they were protected and had opportunities for "better lives". They would guard their territories jealously, maim and kill at any incursion. When a "rule" was violated, the bosses would gather and "talk terms".

When you mentioned those words, "talk terms", in our chat, I had to smile because I knew them. Here was one ex-police officer talking terms with another. What I did not know was how they did it. But you knew. You were there. You had to mediate in one such dispute. I could not believe my ears when I heard you say that. A police officer officiating at a "settlement talk"? It was such a different time, such a different generation.

I was fascinated that these gangs did not demand extortionate sums of money as a "fine" for whatever violation of the gentlemen's code. Instead, they simply asked for 10 tables! Simply tables; nothing more. That was the payment demanded by the aggrieved party. It seemed so trivial when these thugs were used to threatening people's lives on account of "protection money", yet would not inflict that burden on their own kind. Gentlemen's agreement, indeed.

Pa, I have so many questions now about your experiences then. Why had I not inquired further? I was still quite an immature man in his 30s who had failed, at the very least, on the intellectual curiosity front, never mind the simple loving gesture of a son getting to know more about his father. In the words of today, Pa: "Wow, that was *kewl*, my father mediating at a time when the triads practically ruled the people on the ground!"

***

The box was made of bronze, I remember. Beautiful. You kept some of your more treasured possessions in it. In it was another box, much smaller and covered in velvet that retained its beautiful midnight blue, despite the decades. The ribbon was of some satin material. The blue remained vibrant, but the white had turned a grey-yellow with brownish spots covering it unevenly. The one-and-a-half-inch disc was tarnished. I never knew what your medal of bravery was for. How could I not? My own father, who must have risked his life in the line of duty, was awarded such a recognition, and I, his son, never knew the reasons for the medal, and … never asked. I deprived not only you, Pa, of a moment to be proud of your actions, I had also deprived myself of a chance to be proud of my father. It will never come again. No amount of tears or innumerable moments of remorse will ever grant me that opportunity to say to you: "I am so proud of you, Pa." How does one regret what never came to pass? I do not even possess a photo of you and I together.

***

You were a stern father with a gentle smile. I had trouble relating to you even as I saw how you loved us. Was this a legacy from your own distant father, and a mother who favoured her wayward elder son over you? I wanted so much to write about how close you were to your children, how we had many conversations that I could hold onto with affection and laughter, how we did many things together – like in the movies. But, Pa, I see more clearly now, you yourself were caught up in your own world. When I was studying for my degree, the lines from EM Foster's novel, *Howards End*, reminded me of you:

> Only connect! That was the whole of her sermon. Only connect the prose and the passion, and both will be exalted, and human love will be seen at its height. Live in fragments no longer.

I had tried but we could not connect, Pa. The prose and the passion did not connect. It was as if the time had passed and I had already moved on. Yet, what did I move on to that I could not try harder to connect with my own father?

I recall when I was in my mid-teens, you came up and asked me about my future. At the time, I was determined I would join the religious life. Oh yes, I was very much into church and spirituality then, preferring to spend my time doing God's work to being with my family, a misplaced idealism. First, it was with the De La Salle Brothers, then the Discalced Carmelites, before I thought of the Jesuits. My life would be dedicated to the work of God, in and through the church. What were your thoughts then? Were you disappointed at my aspirations? Were you upset that they never came to pass?

There is the one crystal clear moment for me, and I can quote you verbatim, hear your voice, recall your look. You said, in a very firm tone: "Whatever it is, make sure you finish your education first." I did, Pa. I did. Whatever paths I had chosen in life, and there were a few, I had more than completed my basic education. It truly is odd for a man who never appeared to take any interest in his children's studies, or indeed, in their education, that you should have uttered those words to me. Why? What had you seen or experienced in the church or in life that spurred you to keep me grounded in that manner?

I wonder now if you had ever read anything I had written? Certainly, not my poems as you were not that way inclined. I doubt you had read my novel. Did you even know I had written one and won a national prize for it? The very fact I am asking this, Pa, shows how awkward our relationship was. My friends probably know me much more than you ever did. As the Mike + the Mechanics song goes: "It's too late when we die, to admit we don't see eye to eye." Too futile to regret what could have been.

***

In the 80s, the Parish Renewal Experience was all the rage in the archdiocese. It was a programme touted to renew parishes through reinvigorating parishioners. I attended one at the behest of my choir members. I was angsty and emotional, as any teenager would be, then and now. The participants were encouraged to write a letter to a loved one and I thought immediately of you. You got one, Pa, my very first letter to you. I cannot remember the details but I believe it was about how I had felt about us. I recall ending the letter with a plea for you to join the programme, even as I knew it was not the sort of thing you would go to, much less enjoy. It was too talkative. I took that handwritten letter home, and slipped it in your shirt pocket. I had hoped you would participate in the programme because I had wanted to share the experience with you. In my wild teenage imagination, I saw you renewing your faith, but more importantly, taking up the reins of happiness in your life again.

Yes, Pa, deep down, I had always known you were an unhappy man. Marriage did not seem to suit you, painful as it is for me to admit this openly. Divorce was not a choice back then, and not with four children in tow. Would you have taken that route if you had felt it was an option? What about us, your children? Were you so alienated from yourself that you could not connect with us? I had wanted you to take joy in your life, in your family when the teenage me wrote that letter. In the end, in my clumsy way, I alienated the both of us. I never revealed any of my inner thoughts to you anymore after you said no to attending.

Pa, I did not incarnate the words for you, to you. You could not share your inner life with us, but I understood that. You were from a different generation with a different upbringing. Men of your time were meant to be silent, never speaking about their emotions, much less demonstrate them. But I? I had all the training and experience to articulate my feelings and thoughts, and yet … I was the one who was truly locked in, inflexible in my self-righteousness. It would have been easy to blame you for not making those idyllic movies of fathers and sons a reality. And I did, Pa, at one time, but I am unable now, impotent in the face of my hypocrisy. The little wisdom that age kindly bestows on some of us, does not allow me to blame the generation before. I was the one with the power to say it loud, to say it clear, to say it with love and kindness, and I didn't. I failed. If there is an afterlife and you are able to read this, will you forgive me?

***

"My godson." I heard you introducing my foreign partner to your friends as your godson. I was overwhelmed. You accepted him as family, without question. Publicly. And in doing so, you acknowledged me for who I am, no issue, no fights, no confrontation. There was also no awkward conversation; it was all *so* you, the silent Oriental man who did not express his emotions openly, but you did just that. I was ever so grateful, and still am. The conservative Asian man accepted his son's orientation while the progressive *ang moh*'s father just referred to me as my partner's friend for the longest time. For a man of your generation, it was remarkable indeed. I wish I had the wherewithal to thank you then, to tell you in words how much the "my godson" meant to me.

***

I was unreachable because I did not set my mobile phone right, when you were acutely unwell. I returned to my overseas home to frantic messages from my sisters that you were hospitalised. Could not fly out that late evening. Did the next day. Landed. Straight to the hospital in a taxi, luggage in tow. You were already in surgery to remove a blood clot in the brain. In the visitors' room, my elder sister recounted the events, related how she had told you I was coming home to him. She told me you smiled but said nothing. (Were you hoping to see me then?) I cheered up, the whole family did, when the surgeon said the operation was a success.

However, when you could not be awakened several hours later, I had to fight against all my nurse training to cling to that flimsy thread of hope that you will recover. Yes, we could manage with the physiotherapy and rehabilitation. If I had to return to Singapore to help with your care, I would; after all, I was a trained nurse.

***

The one time I saw you cry was when your mother's coffin was shunted into the oven at Mount Vernon crematorium. It was so heartfelt that even if I had wanted to hold back my tears, I couldn't. I cried with you. I cried for you, just as I did when it was your turn to enter that oven. Fire consumes all, except the grief we carry; that will only dissipate with our ashes.

It was cruel to keep you alive when clearly, you had no quality of life. The pressure from relatives was to keep you going. They had read of people waking up from 10 years of vegetative state. The medical consultant was curt, but realistic: The care burden on the family as time went on would have been tremendous. What would have started off as an act of deep love would soon turn to resentment and guilt. The comatose relative would be quietly moved to a nursing facility and the financial demand would drain everyone. Love would not win. Love would not have been sufficient.

I requested the medical consultant to stop the nasal feed. I requested the medical consultant to remove your tracheostomy tube, knowing full well, it was the same as pulling the plug. It was cruel to keep you alive. Was I wrong, Pa? Was I wrong to let you go?

Andrew Koh is an author who has published poems and an award-winning novel, *The Glass Cathedral.* He also has a track record with professional publications in the fields of nursing and Traditional Chinese Medicine. He has worked for over a

Andrew at his work desk.

decade as a registered nurse in London and Sydney. In the latter city, he retrained as a *sinseh*, ran his own Chinese Medicine clinic, and was both a senior lecturer and clinic supervisor for an acupuncture degree programme. While he thoroughly enjoyed practising as an acupuncturist and Chinese medicine herbalist, he has returned to the literary field in education.

To Be A Man

Patrick Sagaram

I do not think you will ever read this letter. Perhaps someone may show it to you by chance. But I will not. You have never read anything I have written. I am afraid you might not like all the things I have got to say. Or you will not know how to talk about them.

I am sure you will not like the men in them.

Except when I sit down to face the blank page, your image floats like a spectre before me as I try to think what it is like to write like a man and be one. If people could see you now, with your skin hanging loosely from your chin, your earlobes long and thin, all they would see is a person shrunken by age. People may see you as you are, but I remember the way you were.

***

One of my earliest memories: In your Datsun 100A, lying on your lap as you drove. I was downing warm Milo out of a bottle, watching sagging power cables pass us like waves. You took me to MacRitchie Reservoir to feed the fishes – I remember that day from the swirl of clouds and sunshine and the midday heat. I must have been just three or four, yet I can recall those fishes thrashing about as we flicked pieces of dried bread into the water, their unblinking eyes like buttons.

Another memory is of you waking me up before first light to go running. You had bought me a pair of white canvas shoes, taught me the right way to tie my laces and we would step out into the chill of the early morning, making our way through the darkness before passing the spice mills, flatted factories and the coffeeshops. In my memory, you were like a shadow over me. You were all shoulders, biceps and strength and I was small, cautious and timid. Even as I grew older, the one thing I could not shrug off was your shadow.

Is it like this for all men, I have often wondered? After so many years, I have come to the conclusion that to be of value to our fathers is often to prove something to them. Except that we all labour under our father's shadow. It is what makes us who we are.

Because you were so exacting and precise in everything you did, you did everything yourself. All the little fixes at home, with the blown bulbs and faulty pipes, you had managed just by a turn of a screwdriver or twist of a spanner which you pulled from your old toolbox. And how about the time you had painted our flat on your own, even working late into the night, as the sweat curved down your back and trickled down your spine. I asked you many times if I could at least hold the paintbrush. But you said no. When I pestered you further, you gave me a look which shut me up.

You had a thing for order and things to be in place. I could not be bothered about mess. You always saw things completed to perfection while I left things done half-heartedly. Your rational side always clashed with my intuitive nature.

Once, I asked you to quit your job and start your own business. I must have been 12 at that time. I knew you were not happy doing what you did. I also knew that you were happiest when you were tinkering around and figuring out a way to make things work. You should have seen that look on your face when my suggestion signalled possibility. But your expression changed almost immediately and you laughed it off as a pipe dream, then told me to stop dreaming.

I could not see the point why someone would continue to spend long hours at work if it left them tired and moody. I could not see the point why someone would not put their youthful energy into trying something new. Of course, it was about money and I knew how strapped we were back then. But more than monetary concerns, I think the fear of the unknown was what kept you from acting to change your life.

And for a long time, it also kept me from acting to change mine. For me, more than the possibility of failure was the scourge of disappointment. But I always imagined how our lives would have turned out if you had taken a chance on yourself. It would have taught me how to do the same. To find something meaningful, we have to lose our way sometimes.

The worst thing in life is dying without realising what you could actually have become. To me, not trying, out of fear, is worse than failure.

We do not always need to make everything fit. Most of the time, we are just groping in the dark, but I think that is the only way we can decide whether to embrace or abandon it. Very few people have the guts to abandon things, especially when they are defined by security and stability – two things which I think you value too much.

I want to tell you that there is no reason why a person cannot abandon a job that does not fit him any longer and to strike out into the unknown for something closer to their heart. Of course, there are risks and the possibility of loss. But the security or stability of a life lived shackled to a routine can destroy one's spirit.

You also showed me that tragedy and suffering will come and there is no escape. No one is ever insulated from either of them. Both will come in their own season and their own time. These things are simply unavoidable.

When tragedy and suffering come swooping down, they are unexpected and we are often caught unprepared. They shatter our tiny boundaries and break our world into pieces. For a time, we are living inside a scream that seems to have no exit, only echoes. Those small cares that seemed so important yesterday become nothing and our daily concerns, petty.

You must have gone through quite dark times in your younger days, I can tell. And the way things turned out in our family, it seemed for a time how immobilising everything was for you.

As I look back, I understand now that you were simply doing what any father would have done. What I have learnt, from my own dark moments, is that these painful times are also opportunities to grow. I know you may never fully understand how this could be but this is true. We all need to embrace such moments in our lives and not see them as cause for despair. Instead, see them as a chance to deepen our experiences.

***

You often confused being male with being a man.

I know that the only TV programmes you ever watched were the news and wrestling show *On the Mat.* In your excitement, you would get carried away and punch the air with both fists or catch an imaginary opponent in a sleeper hold.

In fact, the movies I recalled you had enjoyed all had men with style and swagger. From the enigmatic Yul Brynner, to Steve McQueen's lean, weather-beaten face squinting into the sun in *The Magnificent Seven*, to the patron saint of masculinity, Sean Connery, especially when he starred in *From Russia With Love*. His brutal, bone-crunching fight scene with Robert Shaw on the Orient Express immersed me in a culture in which issues could be resolved by a simple fist to the jaw.

I do not suppose you recall all the cold baths you had subjected me to, knowing how much I had hated them. When I pleaded, you told me to grit my teeth and bear it.

Another thing I had to endure was the coconut oil Ma rubbed into my head. She would use the tips of her fingers to massage the oil into my scalp before running a comb through my hair, making sure it was firmly parted and slicked down.

Back when there was no air-conditioning in the bus, the morning sun came in strong when I was on my way to school. Sweat from my scalp, mixed with the oil, would start to inch its way down the sides of my face. I used to carry a handkerchief just to wipe it off but it was not of much use. By this time, this older boy, Keng Cheong – the one with the glass eye – would say something in Mandarin to his friends and they would roll their heads in laughter and fan their noses at me.

So many times, I had begged you, please, to stop Ma from doing it.

"The oil makes your hair shiny," you said instead, sipping your morning coffee and flipping the newspapers back and forth. "Just ignore them," you said as the words skidded off the roof of your mouth and crashed with a soft explosion.

Maybe it was your way of toughening me. When your nephew Ramesh lived with us, you insisted he take the bed next to the window because you said he was older and that gave him the right. I slept on the mattress on the floor, my head below the family altar, as *Pāṭṭi* (Grandma) insisted, because the other way meant my feet would be pointing at the statue of Jesus and this was disrespectful.

I would lie with my hands behind my back, my feet crossed at the ankles, staring at the rise and fall of the curtains, the slow wind making tiny waves in the cloth. On warm nights, it took forever for sleep to come because mosquitos buzzed around my ears and stung my arms, or a house lizard kept peeling out clicks. Those nights I wished I could trade places with my cousin, so I could shut my eyes instead of listening to him talk in his sleep.

You had a strange way of toughening me up.

And your way of softening my anxiety when I packed my bags for Tekong was only to say how the army would make a man out of me.

Being male is a biological condition, but to be a man is something completely different. We tend to mix up the two, thinking manhood is only about physical strength, aggression and dominance.

I think you figured it out that night when you and *Pāṭṭi* had that blazing fight and she packed her things and left and swore never to set foot in our house again. You did not see it coming. It came out of the blue and threw your world off its axis.

I could tell. Perhaps at that time, you must have realised there are things you cannot settle with brute strength.

After that, you rarely smiled. Ever so often, I would catch you lost in your private thoughts when you stood by the window, the wind fanning your face.

Your anger rang deep and your heart was lonely at its core.

It would be almost 10 years before the two of you would speak again. For the first few months after she left, I could tell your confidence was shattered. *Pāṭṭi* was one of those matriarch types that glued our family together and nobody made any move without her counsel. Even after diabetes had taken away her knee, she was all steel inside. I was there every morning when Ma gave her the needle. Not once I saw *Pāṭṭi* flinch or make a wheezing sound the way you did when you sometimes cut yourself shaving.

When your mood was not good, I would always try and stay clear. It was easy to tell because you had a surly, closed-mouth expression, like you had scalded your tongue or something. Unlike Suresh, who knew how to coax affection out of you even though he is five years younger than me, I was the one always getting into trouble because of something I said. Often, I wondered if it was something I did. I could not tell the difference, really. Your punishments were swift,

I recall. That was why when I was in Primary 6, I wrote an essay about you, titled "Mr Torture", for English class. But my teacher thought I was only fooling around and so made me write another.

(By the way, I could also tell when your mood was good because you would be whistling those Illayarajah (well-known Indian film composer and singer) hits, which played on the radio Ma kept going all day.)

***

You would agree if I told you we did not see eye to eye when I was growing up. My long fringe reminded you of stoned-out hippies and you hated the music I blasted on my stereo each time we went at each other. You could not stand it when I spent all my time kicking a ball or strumming a guitar with the boys at the void deck.

And I could never forget your look when you caught me with a lit cigarette clamped between my fingers when you returned home early from work. I was prepared to get it good from you, except that your look of disappointment was enough to remind me never to do something so stupid again.

Over the years, I have come to count my blessings. I have realised how others have not been so lucky. Their memories of their fathers are filled with the smell of alcohol as a fist came crashing into the side of their face. Or moments spent hiding in corners beneath the sound of broken glass. Or being paralysed by pain after that first burning slap of the belt.

You would laugh with disbelief if I told you how the clutter in the house now upsets me. And now if I cannot seem to do something so exacting and precise, I would choose not to do

Patrick and his Dad.

it. Just the other day, while shaving, I looked into the mirror and it occurred to me how much I look like you. It was like we had bled into each other.

I am glad how much closer we have grown over the years, even if I lack the courage to tell you so. I am glad we have looked past our differences.

***

The sun is coming up behind me as I bring this letter to a close. It is the middle of October, two weeks to your 80th birthday. We had made plans to celebrate. Even Ramesh wanted to drive down from Kuala Lumpur unannounced, just to surprise you. I guess the surprise is on us, given the way things have turned out, with travel restrictions still in place. Guess it is only the four of us.

Outside, a breeze has started up. The branches dance and the flowers turn their faces from the wind. It is going to be a good day.

Patrick Sagaram's work has appeared in *Quarterly Literary Review Singapore* and *Wine & Dine*. He lives in Singapore and works as a teacher.

Man in the Mirror

Loh Guan Liang

To the Man in the Mirror,

Like you, my wife Vivyan cuts my hair in the toilet. I ask her to because it saves money. Mostly, it is because there is little an expensive hairdo (or a cheap one at Snip Avenue, for that matter) can do to save this pate of mine. Like you, lines are starting to lurk at the corners of my eyes, like cracks on a wall. There are furrows in my brow deeper than any line of poetry I can muster. Maybe it is the realisation that the year — and what a year it has been — is coming to a close, or age catching up with me. But these days, I find myself thinking about you more.

Just as how it was with you and your father, I, too, have spent a meaningful amount of time not wanting to be you. I do not know how they do it, but fathers have a knack of leaving traces of themselves in their children so effortlessly. They influence the next generation without even trying. Something about them lingers even after they are gone, like water stains on a glass window. Which can be pretty awesome or awful, depending on what sort of father you have got.

What sort of father does that make you then? I am clawing towards 40 and I still have no clue. You were an unsmiling, uncommunicative man whose idea of father-son bonding was hanging out with your mechanic friends at vehicle workshops. That, or helping you with home repairs. Growing up, I do not think we talked much. Not about things that matter, in any case. It was not that we treated each other like strangers. No. We did talk, sort of…if you consider monosyllabic responses to your commands talking. (Heaven forbid I should ignore you, much less talk back at you!) It never occurred to you to ask if being your assistant around the house was what I wanted. I suppose not. Your scowl made it painfully clear that some things were not my choice to make. Children do what their parents tell them to. That is what makes them precious. Children possess the potential to be what their parents' preferences want them to be. Children are the future.

After all, where else can you find a creature more helpless and dependent on you than your offspring? I mean, seriously.

Case in point: Taekwondo. You loved martial arts so much that I had to too. I was like, what, seven when you sent me for my first Taekwondo class? Or eight? Does age even matter? What is a boy to do when his father puts him in a *gi* uniform and tells him: "Do not fail me"? Fortunately, I grew quite fond of punching and kicking. In fact, I get a kick out of martial arts so much that I still hone my techniques even today.

With Wei, however, it is a totally different story.

Wei went through the wringer like me, but by the time he came along, you had run out of steam. You had big plans for him, but the flesh grew weak. You could not monitor him as closely as you wished you could; your fatigue gave him room to resent you for it. When Wei speaks about you sending him to get punched and kicked, he spits the memory out like poison.

One thing I remember about you is, oddly enough, the smell of your storeroom. Notice I call it *your* storeroom. Fetching you a multimeter from your storeroom was akin to entering a dark forest that smelt of lubricant and stale sweat, with slight notes of heavy grease. Most people I know keep old newspapers and canned food in their storerooms. In your storeroom, however, these items huddle in a corner like refugees while an array of electric drills, cable ties and extension cords look impassively on.

I do not think we have ever exchanged a word of English. You were never the sort of person who would read to your children. If anything, you often insisted I borrow books from the library and read them from cover to cover myself. On the rare occasion we conversed in English, it was with words like "live", "earth" and "neutral". Imagine the sheer wonder when I discovered how words lived double, even triple, lives outside the primary school classroom. For example, "live" is a state of being, of being alive. Live is an occupation of the space that is life, for all to behold. But live is also danger wrapped in red or brown insulation. It sounds childish, I know, but I fancied myself privy to a secret code of home repair jargon that no one in class knew. Looking at language this way made me feel grown-up and, in some singular sense, closer to you.

So, it came to be that your toolbox became my toy chest. Did you know I used to dismantle and reassemble, with varying degrees of success, the hand-me-down toys I had?

Whole afternoons would whizz by with a screwdriver in my hand. Those broken toys were no fun, to be honest. Your tools were. Funny how if you wanted a pair of locking pliers from your storeroom, I knew exactly where to find them. Yet, for the life of me, I could never find the right words to tell you how I feel. I still can't.

As with most things, my flat deteriorates with each passing day. Ceiling lights throb like eyelids, the switch assembly inside the cooker hood rattles like a loose tooth and door hinges cry out for WD-40. It is when something needs fixing that your voice comes back to me with the force and clarity of shared history. My hands can never forget what you had once drilled in me, even if they tried, bound as they are to muscle memory. You would say things like:

- Keep all equipment after you are done. Do not leave them lying about. Clean up the area.
- When dismantling an item, keep all the screws, nuts, bolts, washers and whatever loose bits in one place. Use a bottle cap, saucer, whatever is at hand. That way, you will not lose anything important. Whatever you take apart, make sure to put them back together.
- Always check that the electrical mains are off before commencing repairs. Have you switched off the mains? Are you sure? Electricity is no joke. Go check it again.
- Do not overtighten screws. Be firm, yet gentle. Finger-tight will do. If you turn too hard too fast, you will damage the screw head. When that happens, the screwdriver has nothing to hold onto and you will not be able to drive the screw deeper in or back it out. A screw with a ruined head is a tough thing to remove.

If only you raised your sons with finger-tight force instead of an iron fist. If only. But you cannot unscrew the years. No one can.

Speaking of screws, I forgot to thank you for the toolbox. Wei lugged it over the other day. It would have been nice if you had passed it to me yourself, but given your condition, it was just as well you rested at home. To be honest, I was not expecting a toolbox containing hardware from your storeroom for my birthday. Vivyan must have told you what your tools mean to me (she is more adept at articulating emotions than me). She must have also told you, despite the hurt you had caused the family, part of me still wished to inherit your will, that steely spirit of tempered fire which made me abhor and admire you. You should see my face when I held your spanners and hammers and took in the distinct oily smells of my childhood. There is weight to memory, a physical heft. Some parents pack lunches for their children. You pack toolboxes.

(Vivyan does not know this, but I have been meaning to get a pair of pliers and diagonal wire cutters. Miraculously, you knew.)

But for all the equipment you have, is there one that can mend what you and M did? You once said that one way to remove a stripped screw is to drill into it. Not so deep until you destroy the screw, but deep enough for a screwdriver to probe in and get a grip so you can start turning. In this respect, I do not think we went deep enough. The entire affair has been untouched for so long we do not even know where we stand anymore. Time has corroded the screwhead of your betrayal and there is little else to do but sand down the surface, plaster it over, slap on a fresh coat of paint and move on. Moving on. We are good at that.

In the early days when we discovered the revolting text messages and furtive phone conversations, Ma tried confronting you about them. However, you did what you did best: Keep mum. In silence, you claimed absolution from culpability. You were the victim of a bad office prank. It was all a mistake. If honesty is a door that opens to the truth, you bolted yours and welded it shut. After a while, Ma grew tired of banging. She installed her own door and the two of you became neighbours to each other's silence. To this day, I am still not sure whether you did what we thought you did with M. I do not think Wei cares. Benefit of the doubt? Benefit of the doubt is not a "Get Out of Jail Free" card. I cannot bring myself to give you that, not after hearing her panicked voice at the end of the line when I picked up your phone once. Betrayal is not a game.

Silence. You honestly believe silence can repair pain? Silence is a weapon, not a tool. In our family, silence fixes nothing.

After all that was not said and done, we turned out all right. A little worse for wear, but nonetheless in one piece — you survived your bypass, and me my divorce. We are hard men, you and I: Believers in hard work, hard to get along with, and yet not that hard to understand once you know us deep enough. You know what else is hard? This. Pouring out the years on paper like it is concrete. There is only so much a letter can do. As they say in Chinese, 冰冻三尺非一日之寒. After all these years, there is simply too much ice and too few words between us. Even if we do manage to break ground and bring

A young Guan Liang in the playground with Dad.

to the surface the permafrost of our past, what are we to do with the raw, comatose emotions that are now starting to thaw? We gird our loins, grit our teeth and soldier on. Sometimes the way out of a difficult situation is to live through it.

Such is life. Life is a current. Not just one that keeps icebergs afloat or pulls us out to sea, but one that surges through us. Electricity. In a sense, we are cables, frayed ones at best. Our mettle shows when the going gets tough. Which can be a problem because exposed cables are a hazard. Like all things frayed, we wll break down sooner or later. Time is another word for life and writing to you has reminded me that all life, however electrifying or terrifying, returns to the earth eventually. Once the current that is life has run its course, all that remains is darkness and dust.

Bear with me. I am almost done. Much of the world today revolves around what is replaceable: Shoes, cars, food processors, relationships, even presidents. Strangely enough, repairing an appliance these days costs more than grabbing a new one off the shelf. Never mind that it is only one component that needs replacing; to patch something up implies imperfection, and the modern world will have none of that. Yet our lives are not perfect, and neither are our kin. I cannot choose my upbringing the same way I pick a coffee machine. I also cannot exchange one set of parents for a better one. Maybe I wished I could sometimes, but that's rubbish. We take what we are given, good and bad. Life may give me lemons, but the lemon law does not apply to family. The mirror is right. You are as much a part of me as I am of you.

Your son,
Guan Liang

Loh Guan Liang is the author of two poetry collections: *Bitter Punch* (Ethos, 2016) and *Transparent Strangers* (Math Paper Press, 2012). *Bitter Punch* was shortlisted for the Singapore Literature Prize in 2018. Loh also co-translated Art Studio (Math Paper Press, 2014), a Chinese novel by Singapore Cultural Medallion recipient Yeng Pway Ngon. His poems and short stories have appeared in the *Singapore Memory Project*, The Substation's *Love Letters Project*, *READ! Singapore* and many others. He updates at http://lohguanliang.weebly.com

Love at Arm's Length

Sarah Voon

Dear Dad,

There is just so much I want to say to you, but I know I will never be able to do so face to face. You have always called me emotional and sensitive. I used to see this as a bad thing, but as I grow older, I am starting to see the value in being able to express my feelings.

For one, I am happier – less burdened by the weight that silence often brings. People do not have to second-guess how I am feeling because I am more than happy to share how I feel to them. But with you, things are different.

I am unable to tell you exactly how I feel. Whether it is out of fear of disappointment or just a general feeling of jadedness, I choose to keep mum when I am around you.

So, perhaps you will never really know how I feel. Or perhaps you will have chanced upon this letter to you and finally know how I feel.

You would think as I turn 30 this year, that I would

no longer be seeking your approval or your acceptance. Woe be me then, as I still hope and long for you to really understand me.

Even as I have become a mother myself to a rambunctious boy, I see myself reflected in him, as he claws past the veils of distractions to get my attention. I still do that with you till today.

It is also a strong reminder to myself that I should afford my son the attention he so desperately craves, so he need not ever feel the way I had felt.

Perhaps things look a little different now than they did when I myself was a toddler clinging to your leg and screaming for attention.

Those WhatsApp messages I had sent you, saying: "Hey Dad, how is it going?" That is me, trying to break through the wall that you have put up all these years. But maybe my messages are akin to a paper hammer, banging on that wall, hoping to make an impact while all it does is waste time, barely making a flutter.

So, if you are reading this, maybe I have finally gotten your attention.

The first thing you are thinking is probably that this is a letter written out of hate, but I have none of those feelings for you anymore. I have spent years sorting through that hatred to find that all I am is a little girl who wants her daddy's love and attention.

Despite you being an absentee father, despite every hurtful thing you have ever said or done to me, I am still that little girl who keeps running back to her dad. I have a strong longing for family that you will never understand.

You must think that when I think of you, I do not have any kind thoughts. But you are wrong.

When I think of you, I think of cold winter nights in Beijing, when it was the school holidays in Singapore and we would visit you there. It was the only time we would get to see you in the year. We would be huddled up in a tiny, windowless room just to seek warmth because the heater in your apartment never worked.

I think about egg fried rice and Game Boy cartridges that we would buy from across the street of your apartment for our five-odd weeks' stay in Beijing. I can still smell and taste that egg fried rice in my mind and my mouth will salivate.

No other egg fried rice in the world could compare to that.

I think about the smell of cigarettes so deeply embedded in our clothes at the end of the night, as we would sit through yet another beer night at Sergeant Pepper's bar. Do you remember that place? We would go there all the time. That was my first exposure to The Beatles.

I think of the randomest thoughts I had during those trips to China. There were promises that you would move us over to China and I would get to go to an international school, live in a landed property and have a dog. "I would be the most popular girl in school if I got a new pair of glasses when I move over," I thought to myself.

What a weird thought.

I had such hope back then. I was so young and gullible. I bought every word you said and as the years went by, I continued to hope that one day, you would call up to say it was time for us to pack up our stuff to move to China.

But that day never came.

One year, when you came back to visit us after we had moved to Kuala Lumpur, I remember you brought home a life-size inflatable Hello Kitty robot! It came with a remote control and even played music. It was so futuristic. Not to mention, it was one of the rare gifts you had given me.

You surprised me with it on my birthday and it was not so much the Hello Kitty toy that made me ecstatic that year, but that you were actually around for my birthday. I vaguely remember bragging to all my friends that my dad would be around for my birthday that year. I did not know back that it was not much to brag about.

But my friends, bless their hearts, obliged the 12-year-old me.

Going back even further into my childhood, maybe when I was three or four, I remember the days you would sit down in the living room with me, while Mum prepared a hearty American breakfast for us on Sundays. You would turn on the TV to watch WWE. I grew up with the Undertaker as my favourite TV character.

Because of you, I loved having bacon and eggs for breakfast. Today, it is still one of my favourite breakfast meals. And both you and Mum wonder how I "grew up" to be so *ang moh* in my taste.

Well, let me remind you that you would take me out for fish and chips at some pub in a food court somewhere and let me play while you and Mum knocked back some beers. Another random snippet of this memory is me running my fingers through a thick, red velvet curtain where this bar was.

These memories, of breakfast and fish and chips, became a weekly tradition that stuck with me — a tradition I want to replicate with my son so that he, too, will have fond memories of his childhood. I want him to have that strong sense of family deeply ingrained in him — to make up for everything I never had.

Somehow, a lot of those good memories I had was before *Mei Mei* was born. Before you really left us. Before I knew what was happening. Before we had to move to Kuala Lumpur because Mum just wanted to go home to Malaysia while you continued to call Singapore your home. Before realising that you had left the family.

I had blamed Mum for moving us to Kuala Lumpur and taking us away from you, but I never knew the truth till I was much older.

So, Dad, when I think of you, it is not all bad, because I would not have known bad until I knew what was good. And those were the good old days.

But then, Dad, so much bad had also happened. So much bad that I do not even remember anymore because my mind has chosen to suppress a lot of those memories and just focus on these good ones.

One of the things I do remember most clearly is waiting. Waiting for you. All the time. Waiting for you to call on special occasions... If you remember.

Waiting for you till the wee hours of the night to pull up your car during those once-a-year visits. Waiting for you to ring the doorbell in the middle of the night because you do not have the keys to the house.

Waiting for you in the dead of the night at the stairs of our Potong Pasir maisonette, as you would come home intoxicated.

The waiting was endless and as a child with little concept of time, it felt like forever, night after night. I had to cling onto the hope that you would somehow show up earlier than usual.

Until today, I hate waiting for people. It is a painful reminder of all the years I had spent waiting for you. I am still a light sleeper until today, too. Subconsciously, I am still waiting.

No, I am not waiting for you to come home anymore. But I am still waiting for you to choose us, your kids, for once. For you to finally grasp the real meaning of family.

I might be waiting but I no longer feel as angry or anxious. These days, the feeling that comes in waves is just ridden with sadness.

I think that the sadness is just remnants of the big feelings that the little girl that I used to be had all those years ago, but was always told to keep it in.

I have a lot of questions for you, Dad. Did you ever miss us? When you left? Did you long for us the way we fiercely longed for you?

Did you ever regret walking out on us? Was there ever a moment in your life when you stopped to think: "I had a good life and I should not have walked away"?

Was it always about the marriage breaking down that made you walk away? Or was it that you never wanted kids?

I always remember you telling me that the day I was born, you cried. The day my son was born, I did not cry. I actually felt so numb – I looked at him like I was looking at a stranger. But I love him with such voraciousness that I cannot imagine ever leaving him for a second. So, despite the lack of tears shed, I knew I could never leave him the way you left us.

What about when we were older and we reunited? It seemed like you really wanted me to live with you and integrate with your new family.

But when push came to shove, you always picked them. Is that really your idea of love? Is your idea of family not telling me that my stepbrother was sick for months before he passed away? Is your idea of integration to leave me out of these "family matters"?

I have never really wanted anything from you except your acceptance. But I have been accused many times of wanting your money. That is kind of funny because you do not have a lot of money to begin with.

We are not gold diggers looking to squeeze you of every cent, contrary to popular belief. I do not know who drilled that idea into your head, but it is completely untrue.

We just needed some money to get by and we appreciate every cent that you sent our way. I know that you did your best for us when you could.

But know that even if you did not put me through university or give me my allowance for those three years, I would have still loved you the same.

I would have still wanted the same thing – your love.

I do not know if this feeling will ever fade away or if I will ever look back at myself and think myself silly. But I suppose if after 30 years, I still feel the same way, the next 30 should feel no different.

Speaking of the future, I have thought a lot about it. Specifically, your last days.

Of course, we will not know when your time will be up. But I do spend an inordinate amount of time thinking about those last days of yours, imagining what they would be like.

Will you be alone? Will you be surrounded by the children that you raised, rather than the children you produced?

Will I cry at your funeral? Will I have finally felt your love? Will your new wife even allow us to be there? Will she allow my mother to be there? Will my mother even want to go? Will she even tell us that you have passed? Or will I have to find out through the grapevine, just like I did with my stepbrother?

These questions plague me.

Will you die peacefully? Or will you go out in an ever-dramatic fashion?

I would like to think it would be something dramatic. That is because I have always associated you with drama.

Being around you has always been like walking through a war zone ridden with landmines, never knowing when I would accidentally take a wrong step and end up with my head blown off. Never knowing when I would set you off.

Never knowing if you are in a good or explosively bad mood. Frankly, this has traumatised me quite a bit.

It has rubbed off on my marriage. There is a lot of fear that it will end up like yours. Both your marriages.

Even though you are still married to your current wife, I am not sure I would consider it to be a successful marriage or one that people would wish to emulate.

Your temper is still one of your biggest weaknesses in life. It has pushed people away and it has generated a lot of fear among your loved ones.

Though it is no fault of yours that you were not raised better, it is still emotionally exhausting to be around that.

I know what I am getting myself into when I ask to spend time with you. I actually have to mentally and emotionally prepare myself before and after every meeting.

It has become a habit for me to give myself a pep talk before one of our meetings. To remind myself not to have any expectations. Yet, somehow, I am always left disappointed because I still cannot connect with you after all these years. After all, we had spent the majority of my life apart.

When I moved in with you at 18, I was moving in with a stranger. I had to get to know you, like I would any other stranger… except that you were my father. You had preconceived notions of who I should be and vice versa.

I guess we just never met each other's expectations and I do not think we ever will. Perhaps you believed a daughter should be filial and submissive – a far cry from what my mother raised me to be.

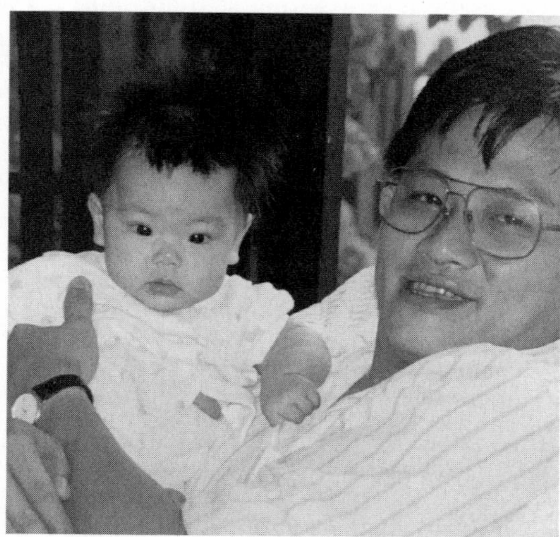

Baby Sarah with Dad.

I believed a father's love should always be unconditional. But things felt very conditional with us. And it still does.

So, I continue to keep you at arm's length and it is truly sad that in this one lifetime on earth, we will never have a functional, healthy relationship. But I have come to (mostly) accept that.

Just know that if one day, you decide to choose me (and my sister) again, we will welcome you back with open arms unconditionally.

Love from afar,
Your eldest daughter.

Sarah Voon has been in the media publishing industry for almost a decade and is now the General Manager of *theAsianparent Malaysia*. Though she was born and raised in Singapore, she calls Malaysia home and identifies as a true-blue Malaysian foodie. When she is not being a full-time corporate flyer, she devotes every waking second to her miracle of a son. Fun fact — his name is Jedi.

The Reply

Koh Jee Leong

You're silent now, and it's no surprise,
you've been a silent movie all my life.
That's poetry's way of putting it, and it's
dead wrong—you're no Chaplin, funny
and glamorous, although you may be
one of the mini-minions in *Metropolis*.
No, you're not the proof for a thesis.

My earliest memory is riding on your
shoulders heading home from the merry-
go-round. My last memory, of you living,
your lung walls succumbing to the flooding,
is the speechless and tearless hospital bed,
and me planting a kiss on your forehead.
Between these short clips, you bicycling
down the gentle swerve of road that hugs
the bottom slope of Mount Faber like a rug,

me sitting with my pianica on the top tube,
legs slightly raised to free the circling pedals.

We're a home movie that nobody wants
to watch, except the family, the ones
knowing, sentimental, and disputatious.
Your four brothers, rich with arrogance,
your two sisters, hard as stale biscuits,
expect you to agree with them, and you do,
backpedalling as you do. There's the rub.
I see it and judge it craven of you,
not seeing then I am your best reply,
what with my school honours and, eventually,
my scholarship to go overseas.

While mother hogs the weekly phone calls
with talk of winter clothes and shopping malls,
your silence grows and grows on me, profound
as the first snow falling on college grounds.
At the end of time, three long, exciting years,
out of Heathrow mother and you appear
and I'm shocked to see the snow in your hair.
Loveliest of trees, the cherry now
is hung with bloom along the bough...

To my flowering regret, you've flown the distance
but I deny you the pomp and circumstance.
Thinking myself above empty ceremonies
and you and mother below the Latin service,

I don't sign up for the Sheldonian show,
but throw together an improvised shoot
of us in the college garden, me geared up
and you gamely following this young pup.
Not a word of reproach, not a subtitle,
my Joe pays off his Pip's unpaid bills.

You won't know the reference, but you
would like Joe, both of you working men,
he a blacksmith and you an electrician,
both of you surviving shits for fathers
with your goodness intact, saving dicks
for sons with your belief in the best of larks.
There I go, showing off my learning
and irreverence, there I go again,
poetrying. I'm still answering my aunts
and dear uncles, who are dying, dead,
or softening to the middle of their heads.

It's worsening, since living in New York,
I've written book after book after book,
and placed them like bombs in your hands.
You keep them carefully by your bible,
in the high drawer of the TV cabinet,
the cheek by the turn-your-other-cheek.
Where is strength? Where is weakness?
What is truly evil? What is goodness?
The freedom fighter's someone's terrorist,
someone's draft dodger the pacifist.

This week my XI's read the Oedipus
and, like all generations, were nonplussed
by the enormities wrought by right intent,
fleeing father-murder to father-murder,
abjuring mother-sex to sleep with her.
If to save a baby is to kill all babies
through the lightning plague in the city,
what should we do with the mewling
mess, milk-stained, exposed, ankle-torn,
on the green, wooded slopes of Kithairon?
There are some places like Singapore
that would make the careful calculation.
There are some places like Greece, once,
that would pose the question and no more.
You, my father, are the Grecian oracle.

There I go again. This habit of reading life
as if it's a work of art, this tendency,
grows from the library books devoured
tenderly on the walk home while avoiding
the lances thrusting up like lampposts.
And you encourage me, give me courage—
when at the books corner you leave me
and shop with mother, for life, at OG,
you show me, as an unschooled man's able,
you're replaceable and irreplaceable.

At your wake, attended by relatives
and a number of poet-friends, I give

the reply of the living to the dead.
For you, looking oddly like bread
in the yellowing husk of your body,
the eulogy begins with the bicycle,
and it says, I remember, I remember.
Just that. All the carefully chosen
phrases reducible to one refrain.

But a letter is not a eulogy — it has
much more of me in it and, at last,
much more of you, my father, in me.
When you're loaded into the oven,
to lift from us the annual burden
of visiting and sweeping your grave,
I'm seized by a wild desire to swear
that before every poetry reading, I'll say,
I'm Koh Jee Leong, the son of Koh Dut Say,
in the manner of the Malays and others.

The desire passes. Let this be the brother,
the guilty brother, to the dead and gone,
the reply a replacement for other ones,
the movie you and I've together caught,
the son you have for the sons you have not.

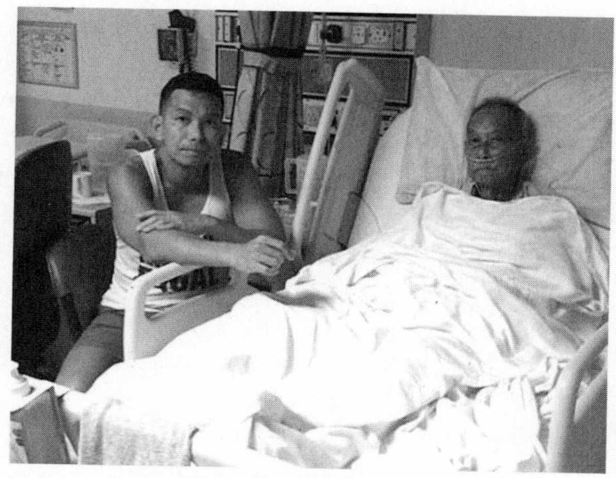

Jee Leong visiting Dad in the hospital.

Koh Jee Leong is the author of *Steep Tea* (Carcanet), named a Best Book of the Year by UK's *Financial Times* and a Finalist by Lambda Literary in the US. He has published four other books of poems, a volume of essays, and a collection of *zuihitsu*. His latest book, a hybrid work of poetry and prose, is *Snow at 5 PM: Translations of an insignificant Japanese poet.* Koh lives in New York City, where he heads the literary non-profit Singapore Unbound and the indie press Gaudy Boy. https://singaporeunbound.org/

Other books in the series

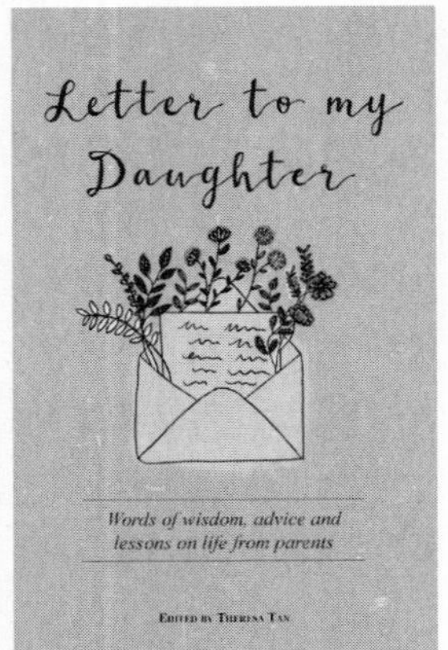

Featuring contributions by Adlena Oh-Wong, Amy Poon, Ng Choong San, Cynthia Chew, Dawn Lee, Dawn Sim, Janet Goh, Jennifer Heng, Jenny Wee, Kalthum Ahmad, Karen Tan, Landy Chua, Loretta Urquhart, Paige Parker, Petrina Kow, Sangeeta Mulchand, Shaan Moledina-Lim, Chiong Xiao Ting, Lin Xiuzhen, Yen Chua and Zalina Gazali

Featuring contributions by Anitha Devi Pillai, Anthony Goh, P N Balji, Bernard Harrison, Chris Henson, Christopher Ng, Clement Mesanas, Daniel Yap, Darren Soh, Dinesh Rai, Fong Hoe Fang, Gilbert Koh, Kenny Chan, Lester Kok, Mark Laudi, Nizam Ismail, Olivier Ahmad Castaignede, Roland Koh, Sanjay Kuttan, Vicky Chong

Featuring contributions by Christine Chia, Regina De Rozario, Tania De Rozario, Charmaine Deng, Nanny Eliana, Gwee Li Sui, Beverly Morata Grafton, Sharda Harrison, Lydia Kwa, Jo-Anne Lee, Faith Ng, Irene Ng, William Phuan, Martha Tara Lee, Rose Marie Sivam, Cheryl Charli Tan, Jean Tan, Wahid Al Mamun, Georgette Yu, Zuraidah Mohamed